VESSEL OF CLAY

VESSEL OF CLAY

❧

by *LEO TRESE*

SHEED & WARD

NEW YORK

1950

NIHIL OBSTAT

    LEON O. KENNEDY
    Censor deputatus

IMPRIMATUR

    ✠ STEPHEN S. WOZNICKI
    Vic. Gen.

Detroit, February 1, 1950

To the "Little People" of Christ's Church:

THE LAITY

whose love and reverence for their priests make us
so often ashamed of falling so far short
of their just expectations.

Contents

Six Thirty	*page*	1
Seven O'Clock		4
Seven Thirty		7
Seven Fifty-five		10
Eight O'Clock (I)		14
Eight O'Clock (II)		18
Eight O'Clock Plus		21
Eight Forty		24
Nine O'Clock		27
Nine Fifteen		31
Nine Thirty		35
Nine Forty-five		39
Ten O'Clock		43
Ten Fifteen		47
Ten Thirty		51
Ten Forty-five		55
Eleven O'Clock		59
Eleven Forty-five		63

Twelve O'Clock   *page*   67
One O'Clock   70
Two O'Clock   73
Two Fifteen   77
Three Thirty   81
Four O'Clock   85
Five O'Clock   89
Six Fifteen   93
Six Thirty   97
Seven Thirty   100
Eight Thirty   104
Nine Thirty   107
Ten Thirty   110
Eleven Thirty   113

VESSEL OF CLAY

6:30

ONE HAND GROPES for the alarm clock, two feet hit the floor. Another victory is achieved; another day begins.

Sometimes I have felt that a priest's salvation is determined during those first ten seconds after Big Ben sounds his call. It is so easy to say to oneself, "Just five more minutes." The five minutes become fifteen or thirty, and then there is a quick splashing of water and a mad dash for the altar. The day's work starts, with nothing more than the vesting prayers to give it pace and meaning.

Strangely enough, we can repeat that performance morning after morning, without perceiving the childishness of it. We set the alarm one hour in advance of Mass as a half-hearted salve to our consciences; we will not admit even to ourselves that we really have no intention of getting up at that time.

It is not this way with everyone, but it was this way with me for a long time after I left the seminary. As I fit a new blade to the razor (there's far more lift in a clean-shaven face than in ten minutes extra sleep), my thoughts go back to those early days as a priest. It puzzles me now to understand how I could so often have over-slept, more than once keeping the people waiting for Mass. I cannot understand why I did not perceive the spiritual softening and weakening that lack of prayer brought in its train. It amazes me to think that I could ever have been content with a hastily formed intention as I walked from rectory to sacristy.

This sounds like the reminiscing of a self-righteous prig. But I do not mean that I am a good priest, even now. I only mean that I have been a worse one. In all probability I should have been a much worse one, but for the act of God and my Bishop which made me pastor of my own small parish where I had to give the Sisters Holy Communion an hour before Mass. On an empty stomach the morning paper and the radio have no appeal for me. So, with an hour to kill, I settled down at a *prie-dieu* in the sanctuary, and life began—at thirty-four.

(As I dry my face and give my head a quick rub, I reflect that I shall never be canonized; they will find hair-tonic in my medicine cabinet.) Now why did I have to wait for nine years to learn something that I should have realized when I left the seminary? I had had the necessity of prayer drummed into me, but I wasn't, apparently, convinced of it; I wasn't sold on it. Perhaps the seminary's sheltering walls gave us a false feeling of confidence. We left those walls under an initial impetus administered from without . . . and we thought it was spiritual energy driving from within. The hard part was over; we could ease up now; we could coast along. We had heard of fallen-away priests, of course, but somehow they didn't seem any more real than Martin Luther. We didn't visualize them as having once been young priests like ourselves, equally self-confident—cocky is perhaps the word.

Why is it that we leave the seminary, grown men of

twenty-four or more, still in the formative stage? One is tempted to wonder (I'm only ruminating, of course, as I button my cassock) whether the seminaries couldn't do a better job of making us into adults before ordination. I do not mean that the *neo-ordinatus* should not be childlike, with the simplicity of a clear conscience. I mean that he should not be childish in the approach to duties and the acceptance of responsibilities.

(A whiff of fresh morning air greets me as I open the door. The lilacs by the side porch are almost in bloom.) The "curfew" rules for assistants, effective in many rectories, seem a tacit admission of failure somewhere along the line. I don't mean that the curfew rules aren't necessary. But am I wrong in thinking that they *shouldn't* be necessary?

(The convent door is ajar for me. It is seven o'clock and the Sisters are waiting.) I'm glad I'm not a bishop or a seminary rector. Just the same, I wish there were some way to start us out in life with a more solid piety and a better-developed sense of responsibility. I wish we didn't have to learn so much the hard way.

7:00

THE CONVENT DOOR is on the latch. As I close it behind me, I hear the clock strike seven. The Sisters are waiting. Yes, I think, as I climb the stairs to the chapel, the Sisters are waiting. They spend a good part of their lives in waiting for, and waiting on, us priests. They wait for us in the morning as we come to give them Holy Communion or to offer their Mass. They wait for us in the classroom, with catechism and class-roll opened and ready for us on the desk. They wait for us on their confession day. They wait for us to examine the altar boys and to read the report-cards and to order the candles and to wash the purificators.

As I hurriedly slip into surplice and stole, it is with a guilty consciousness of all the precious minutes I have wasted for the Sisters. The times I've kept them waiting through necessity could be counted on the fingers of two hands. The times I've kept them waiting through negligence and thoughtlessness would need computing on an adding machine. Few hours are so carefully planned, and no minutes so usefully expended, as those of the Sisters. And yet if someone must wait, if someone's schedule must be disrupted, well, "the Sisters won't mind" is a phrase that settles everything.

One of the priesthood's baffling mysteries is how we

dare to patronize these women whose sanctity, whose zeal and ability, often exceeds our own. Our facetious references to "the good nuns" or to "Mother Abbess" may inflate our ego, but there must be wincing in Heaven at the ingratitude of priestly hearts. If there were table-talk among the Saints, surely a high-ranking topic would be: "How do priests get that way?"

Certainly Sisters are human; impeccability is not one of their attributes. We can go farther and admit that sometimes superiors are lacking in prudence and judgment. That is evident. Only a highly imprudent superior would make a request, for example, where the choice must lie between Father's comfort and the Sisters' convenience. Only a foolhardy nun would hint that something should be done that Father hasn't already thought of; only a moron would expect Father to give a reason for decisions that to the uncharitable-minded might seem capricious and inconsistent.

My mind is not on the "O Sacrum Convivium" as I recite it. I am recalling that my own vocation (and that of many another priest) is due, under God, to the inspiration, the encouragement, and the prayers of nuns. Well do I know that my crowded church and busy communion railing are due to no eloquence of mine; it is the long and weary classroom labor of bonneted heads that has breathed reality into the Christian life and sacraments. It's a wonderful feeling to have the boys doff their caps on the street with a "Good morning, Father"; it's most satisfying to have the garage man say, "Oh, no, Father, I wouldn't charge you for that"; it's very flattering to have the cop on his motorcycle say, "Sorry, Father, I didn't know it was you." Where did they learn their veneration for the priesthood? Not in the rectory office. Sister Euphemia taught them that in the fifth grade.

"*Benedictio Dei Omnipotentis* . . ." We priests, it would seem, need to see the Sisters as human beings with a family background and their own personal traits. They are not automatons without feelings or sensibilities. They do not claim to be saints. Successes are just as welcome to them, disappointments are just as keen to them, and praise is just as sweet to them, as to us. More so, in their circumscribed and (even though divinely) regimented life. For all their angelic gaiety as Father visits them in their recreation room, they just can't be superhuman all the time. They have their headaches, too. They have their black moments, and with no housekeeper or janitor to work it off on.

As I blow out the candles, I wonder what started me on this line of thought? Well, maybe my conscience can stand stirring, even if I haven't snapped at one of them lately. Today when I go into the school I must be sure to tell Sister Francelin how well she has the altar-boys trained; I must remark on the immaculate altar-linens to Sister Elmyra; I must compliment Mother Grace on the splendid discipline in her classroom. Leaving the chapel, I feel so paternally beneficent that I actually smile at Mother as she raises her head for a moment from her thanksgiving. I can see that she is puzzled, but she smiles bravely back. Father is always so right.

7:30

ONE SOLID SHOVE transfers me from kneeling-bench to chair, and the shortest half-hour of the day begins. Time was when even a fifteen-minute meditation was an heroic act—something to be omitted with little excuse and no sense of loss. It seems too bad that it took me so long—I stoop for the marker as it falls from my book—so long to discover that what they told us in the seminary about meditation is all true. About it being so necessary, I mean; and such a well of strength besides. The trouble was, I still hadn't learned to meditate, even at the end of fourth theology. I still was so tangled up in preludes and compositions of time and place and person and practical applications and spiritual nosegays, that I never quite got around to meditating. The stage-directions were plain enough: the parts to be played by memory and imagination and intellect and will. But somehow it was such a distraction to be on the alert for the cues; and, as likely as not, the suddenly summoned faculty just stood around, as uncertain as I what to do next.

My thumb creases back the pages of Fr. Leen's *In The Likeness of Christ.* (I'm a book meditator, and always will be; one of those undisciplined minds that needs to be firmly tethered while it does its grazing. The texts of Tanquerey and Parente afford all that I know of contemplation, sadly I confess.) My thoughts seem unusually skittish this morning, but Fr. Leen soon will provide the bell-wether to bring them into line. It may take a paragraph, it may take two or three pages, but I know that something will strike me between the eyes. Some sentence will jump out of the page and say, "This is for you, friend," and conscience will take over from there.

What I like about Fr. Leen or Abbot Marmion or Dom Chautard is that they aren't always sneaking up and shouting, "second point," or "third point," just as one is beginning to see a glimmer of truth in the first point. I wonder who started that three-point business, anyway? True enough, in the seminary we expressly were told that if one point is meaty enough, we should stay with it. Yet every morning in chapel it was three points we got, and no "meditation book" is complete without them. How others may be I cannot say, but my own soul seems to freeze up at the sight of preludes and points marshalled in careful array.

If I were spiritual director in a seminary—well, to begin with, I should perish of fright at the mere prospect. Only think of the flame that must blaze in the heart of the director if he is to kindle all the torches in the choir-stalls about him! But if I did labor under such awful responsibility, I think I should strive to eliminate the reading of formal and set meditations as a community exercise. If a book had to be used, I should use it to fortify myself in private, then meditate aloud with my brethren.

What a one I am to be talking about meditation! I hear the altar-boys coming into the sacristy, whispering carefully so as not to disturb me—and I haven't even started. I can't blame *that* on the seminary. Nor a lot of other things. It's not the seminary's fault that I succumbed so early in my priesthood to the heresy of good works: late hours spent in young people's activities, for example, with consequent late rising and token prayers. I excused myself with the thought of the "wonderful influence" I was having on the youth of the parish, forgetting that God's little finger could accomplish more than all my excited hustling. My vanity made mockery of His grace, while the angels trembled, I am sure, at my brashness.

No use to blame the seminary, either, for my stupendous self-confidence. All those warnings that had been dinned into us about pitfalls and dangers; what was all the shouting about, anyway? Why, it was easy to be good. All one had to do was to keep busy. To keep busy. To keep busy. . . . So I thought.

Oh! Oh! There comes the server out to light the candles, and where is my meditation? Well, forgive me, dear Lord, this once, this once again. And let a bruised reed offer a prayer to Your Sacred Heart for the straight young shoots that are rising to replace us. Teach them, convince them—and if their skulls are as thick as mine, *pound it into them*—that they'll be of no use to You, whatever their talent, unless they drink deep of Your Spirit each morning.

7:55

FIVE MINUTES to eight by the sanctuary clock. As I hoist myself to my feet, a final moment of resolution concludes the morning's meditation. In the sacristy the altar boys are waiting for me—red-headed Don, whose hands as usual display a liberal layer of mother earth; and freckle-faced Jimmy, who has fought his customary losing battle with a mop of wiry hair. "Good morning, Father," they chorus, in answer to my greeting. My own Lavabo completed, and Don put to work on his with a cake of soap, I pick up the amice. "*Impone, Domine*," I begin, but before the prayer is finished the gremlin who so often rides my thoughts has taken over again.

This time the subject is altar boys. Don there behind me, leaving black imprints on the towel to break the sacristan's heart, thinks he wants to be a priest. He's only an eighth grader, and a lot can happen in twelve years, but maybe he *will* be one of the answers to my daily memento for abundant vocations from this parish. If the priestly vocations don't come from among the altar boys, then where else shall I look? Who is more apt than they to hear the Voice of invitation from the tabernacle?

"*Dealba me, Domine*"—but the gremlin still rides: I am remembering again that God is at least as much interested as the Holy Father or myself in seeing that His Church is blessed with sufficient vocations. Sufficient, did I say? Profuse would be a better word, considering the liberality of a God Who drops a thousand acorns that one oak may grow. If the vocations are not coming to fruition, where lies the fault? A little chill of self-doubt chases itself down my spine as I tighten the cincture. The usual glib excuses offer no escape: lax Catholic homes and pleasure-mad environment. I've tried those refuges before, and they offer poor shelter. For who, more than myself, is responsible for laxity or materialism in my flock?

I may as well face it. If this parish doesn't produce its fair share of priestly vocations, the responsibility will lie at my door—no other. It will mean that I am not cultivating the seed that the Lord has planted. What is it that the theologians say—"grace follows nature"? Something like that, anyway. If God's semination is to be effective, the soil must be prepared and enriched, the first tender shoot must be nurtured and cared for.

As I pick up the maniple, I wonder how well I'm discharging my job as vocation husbandman. If boys are to be attracted to the priesthood, then the priesthood must be made attractive to them; "that's for sure," as Jimmy would say. The whole point is that "priesthood" is a meaningless abstraction for these boys. To them, I am the priesthood. If they like what they see in me, the Master's call will come much more clearly to their ears. Do they see in me the supernaturalness of the priesthood? Do they find me kneeling in prayer before the altar when they come to serve—even when they arrive half an hour early? Do they see me there again, in thanksgiving, when they leave?

Well, yes. But that's not enough—as I fasten stole with

cincture. Kids' ideals are so *darn* high, and their instincts so perceptive. They've heard for example of the gentle charity of Christ, and I know that unconsciously they'll measure me against it. That's one reason for my cheerful, "Good morning, boys," before Mass, and the "Thank you, boys," after Mass. It's the reason, too, for the careful guard I try to place over my impatience, so that their human errors, their thoughtlessness, their awkwardness, may not bring a stinging and un-Christlike rebuke from my lips. That's why correction must be venomless, and praise generous.

"*Domine qui dixisti*" is accompanied by a bit of a sigh. There are so many ingredients that go into a vocation, and I dare not leave any out. If the boys are to know more of the priesthood, they've got to know more of me. That's why, long since, I took over the training and direction of the servers myself. They aren't nearly as polished as when good Sister Ludwig was their mentor, but there is more of a "togetherness" as they and I offici-ate at the altar. No excuse now (was there ever?) for turning around at the "*Hanc igitur*," with a sibilant "Ring that bell!" They correct their own mistakes and air their problems in the easy informality of our weekly meeting.

In one little thing I can take comfort (the clock says one minute to eight): the altar boys aren't afraid of me. I never could see that there was any necessary connection between "sacred" and "scared," similar though the words may look. That anyone at all should be "scared" of the priest is a horrible enough thought; that there should be fear of him in the hearts of those who freely give their time to assist him at the altar is doubly unthinkable. Re-spect for holy things there must be, and reverence in the sacristies. But if Eddie Higgin's exuberance bubbles over, and he chooses to tell me just before Mass that he's got a new baby sister—well, I cannot conceive that Christ is frowning, nor do I.

Even the so-called natural elements that may help along a vocation, I must not ignore. This thing called "hero-worship," for example, that plays such a large part in every kid's life. It's hard to compete with a lad's favorite ball-player or cowboy star, but I can try. Which accounts for our frequent swims together in the summer, a football game in the fall, a hockey-game or a movie in the winter. In my small parish, with a dozen or so servers, such outings aren't difficult. And I'm never tempted to feel that I'm wasting time that could be put to more useful purposes; what *could* be more useful than another priest—except two or three?

The clock has caught me napping, with all this ruminating. Half a minute after eight, and time to be going. As I pick up the chalice and bow to the cross, it occurs to me that Vocation Clubs are effective, not because of formal organization, but because they get the priest directors doing what all of us ought to be doing all the time —laboring might and main to fill our ranks. The ringing of the sacristy bell catches me with a prayer upon my lips: that no vocation may go unheeded or unanswered because I, by word or example or neglect, have failed to give full amplification to the Voice of God.

8:00 (I)

IT DOESN'T TAKE long to unfold the corporal and to open the Missal upon the altar. But it doesn't take long, either, for the host of distractions that seem to lie in wait for this most holy Action of the day to swing to the attack. They come like dive-bombers that have been waiting in ambush behind a cloud. Even as I check the Missal markers I realize that the daily battle between distraction and devotion has begun. Even the pattern of it all can be forecast. There will be a brave start at the foot of the altar, and about the time that I have finished my confession of guilt before all the Court of Heaven, suddenly I shall remember that I forgot to phone the Holy Name speaker about the change in meeting dates. (The servers will give me plenty of time to solve that difficulty. I have dinned into them that their responses are an integral part of the Mass, and must be read—I don't trust their memories—slowly and reverently. By the time their clear and careful voices have finished the *Confiteor*, I shall have the Holy Name speaker disposed of.)

There will be a brief moment of recollection, perhaps, as I appeal, *Ostende, Domine*, for the mercy of a God Whom I forget a moment later as my corn gives a jab of pain while I ascend unto the altar of God. Even as I kiss the relics of the martyrs whose blood has been mingled in sacrifice with that of Christ, I shall be wondering whether it might not be well to try those new corn plasters I saw advertised in the drug store yesterday.

And so the august Sacrifice will proceed, through half an hour of triumph and failure. There is no time of the day, no time of one's life, when the sublime and the petty stand in such startling contrast as now. Worrisome thoughts, vain thoughts, silly thoughts; and now and then perhaps a thought that seems to come straight from the noisome depths of hell; all of them vying with the beauty of the Preface or the solemnity of the *Communicantes* or the plaintive pleading of the *Pater Noster*.

Here is the one moment of the day that justifies my existence as a priest. Anyone can organize societies, anyone can teach catechism, anyone can baptize; yes, and a hundred people in the parish can pray better than I. God's grace can convert sinners, win heretics, and make saints without any help from me. But for these thirty tremendous minutes that are eternal, God *needs* me; only *I* can offer sacrifice;—and I shall stand at the altar reflecting that Polish sausage and sauerkraut would be good for tonight's dinner!

Well, the cure is obvious. A deeper spirit of prayer is certainly the answer. The saints weren't bothered this way. Or were they? All the Saints' Lives that I've read tell of ecstasies at the altar, and rapt radiance of countenance. But maybe the Lives don't tell us of all their Masses. Maybe they had their difficulties, at times. There's comfort in the reflection, anyway. There's momentary comfort, too, in the thought that I'm still in the purgative way, so what else can I expect? A momentary comfort that is quickly vanquished by a twinge of conscience which says that I've tarried there too long.

It isn't that I haven't tried to do something about it. I have overcome the bad habit of my younger days, when a crowded week-day Mass schedule pressured me into a too-fast and too-slovenly pronunciation of the Latin. Mine is not an agile tongue, and it took many months of careful effort to return to preciseness and exactitude in such things as the *Labavo inter innocentes* and the Last Gospel. Often have I envied nimble-speeched confreres for whom a twenty-minute Mass is no effort at all. No doubt their thoughts keep pace with their racing consonants; mine never could.

But deliberateness alone is not enough, not for me. The psychologist's dictum that the human mind cannot concentrate on one point longer than six seconds finds perfect exemplification in myself. My defense has been to erect, here and there through the Mass, anchor-posts at which I can grab as my vagrant thoughts tumble me along. One sure moment of attention on which I can count comes in the *Gloria's* triumphant conclusion: *Tu solus Sanctus, tu solus Dominus, tu solus Altissimus, Jesu Christe.* Wherever my thoughts may be, they seem to hasten back to stand for one majestic moment in the presence of the King. Another such moment comes with the *Benedictus:* it doesn't seem possible to think of anything else as one's arm swings up to the cruciform salute, *Benedictus qui venit in nomine Domini.* The rhythm, the action, the awful solemnity of the Consecration are almost proof against distraction. Almost, but not quite. More than once I have been grateful for a pre-Mass intention carefully formed. Another pre-Mass "must" for me is the careful enumeration of all my personal mementoes for the living and the dead; the Missal's commemorations *pro vivis* and *pro defunctis* so often prove a trap for a vagrant mind. But wander as it will, my attention seems to be caught up sharply by the *Pater Noster*, with its appeal for the coming of His Kingdom and the doing of His Will. So will go my Mass this morning. I shall fall often, to rise briefly. Resolutions will break, fallen nature will be stubborn, yet all defects will fail to shake the hope that is mine as I rise from my knee to proclaim that *Vidimus gloriam ejus, gloriam quasi Unigeniti a Patre.*

There is a sound behind me. The altar boys are stirring. God forgive me, how long have I been standing here like a hypocrite with my head bowed before the crucifix! It is almost with a sigh that I descend the steps. I love my Mass. It is a dark and an empty day that must start without It. But the angels about the altar often must wish that they could push me aside and take my place, as they see me dreaming of tomorrow's ball game, the while their God and mine awaits my summoning word. Well, maybe today I can be just a little more attentive, a little more devout. . . . *"Introibo ad altare Dei. . . ."*

8:00 (II)

THE ALTAR BOYS have been dreaming again; they missed my signal at the end of the Epistle. As I bow in the middle of the altar for the *Munda cor meum*, there is a scuffling and skidding of feet behind me, and a young whirling dervish comes up to grab the book. He'd *better* hurry, I think to myself impatiently. And then I think again. After all, what *is* the hurry? The Mass isn't a radio program, to be timed for a split-second finish. Better not let myself get in that frame of mind again. It was too hard to get out of it last time.

Looking back now, I wonder how I ever got into the habit of saying Mass as though the devil was riding my alb-tail. Come to think about it, maybe he was. It was an insidious development surely enough, from the early days of my priesthood when the Mass was something to be savored and loved, to that later period when speed meant more than beauty. I wince now as I recall how willy-nilly I used to choose the "Black Mass" because it was shorter; how I used to grow impatient if the choir were slow in finishing the *Kyrie;* how I felt a tiny inner resentment if the orations were multiplied or if the Mass called for a *Credo*.

It doesn't seem possible, but there it was. Probably my movements and discharge of the ceremonies kept pace with my false sense of urgency. No one ever told me that I was destroying the solemnity of the Mass by my nervous speed, but of course no one would tell me. I can see myself now, doing a neat swivel for a quick *Dominus vobiscum*, my chasuble billowing in the breeze. I can remember (wish I couldn't) closing the Missal to finish my last *Per omnia saecula saeculorum* at the middle of the altar, and ending the Last Gospel on my way down the altar steps.

Strangely enough, it was a man from another parish, a man who never even saw me say Mass, who brought me up sharp. He was telling me how much he liked to assist at Father Quamprimum's Mass. "Boy O Boy," he said, "you ought to see him say Mass, Father. Mass, sermon, and Communions, and it's all over in twenty-five minutes. That's the Mass for me!" Well, he made the remark with a facial expression that I can define only as a leer. I am humbly grateful that I had enough priestliness about me to feel slightly nauseated at the smirk on his face. And then, like a delayed-action bomb, my ego felt the blow: "I wonder if they'll be saying that about me some day? Dear God, I wonder if they're saying that about me *now!*"

By the grace of God another blow, the knock-out punch, came soon after. A man of my own parish, one of those sterling Catholic fathers, told me how much he enjoyed assisting at the Mass of the visiting missionary. There was no malice in his words, but I could not escape the unintentional implication when he said, "I love to see Father M. say Mass; he makes you feel that every bit's important, and I can follow him so easily in my Missal." And here I had been silently criticizing Father M. for what I considered his over-deliberateness!

Well, I slowed down, but it wasn't easy—not at first. It wasn't easy to substitute precise enunciation for slurred syllables and swallowed consonants. It took time to co-ordinate each action with the words it was supposed to accompany. At first I was just a little troubled by a statement of Father Faber which I had once read—that a conscious effort to say Mass slowly is not devotion; it means we are thinking of ourselves more than of Jesus. Eventually I awoke to the fact that the obverse is equally true —that if we love Jesus the Mass will pace itself accordingly; the predella never will become a race-course.

Just last evening I sat in for a little while on our C.Y.O.'s play rehearsal in the parish hall. The director was hammering at the cast to slow down, slow down. "You think you're moving slowly," he told them, "but out here in front you all seem to be in a hurry. Remember that if your actions are to look normal to the audience, they've got to seem exaggeratedly slow to you— until you get used to it." The Mass is a drama too, I thought to myself. It would be good for me if there were a director in the pews to tell me off occasionally.

But the boy is standing by the book, waiting for me to get on with the Gospel. He's breathless, but triumphant that he's beaten me to the corner. Little does he know, as he pipes, *Et cum spiritu tuo*, of the tiff with impatience that was fought and won as he made his hurried circuit.

8:00 ✝

Memento, Domine, famulorum famularumque tuarum. . . . This is the moment of the Mass when I can gather strength and comfort for the day. I wonder—as I fold my hands and bow my head—whether other priests experience those same blue moments: times when the consciousness of the vast work to be done and the realization of my own inadequacy seem to press upon me like a hopeless burden; times when it seems that I am plowing a forty-acre field with a toothpick; times when a sense of frustration seems to sap initiative and stifle priestly ambition. I suppose that such moments of depression might be written off neatly as due to glandular disturbances or hormone deficiencies—if it weren't that it is faith which so obviously is lacking. After all, who's saving souls, myself or He? What if I do seem to batter myself futilely against a stone wall; what if I do pull a boner or make a wrong guess? *He* doesn't need me to accomplish His purposes. It's only a child who wants to see his homework with "100%" neatly pencilled at the top.

Memento, Domine. . . . Yes, now is the moment when worry seems petty. Now is the time when errors are righted and failures are snatched from the scrap-pile. The Mass is pouring out its inexhaustible torrent of grace before me. I just can't bring forward enough intentions to stem its flow. But time is so short; "a little while" doesn't allow for much. All I can say is, "For all the intentions, Lord, which I mentioned to You in my morning prayers." It is a long list, whose established pattern undergoes daily additions and modifications.

"For all the intentions of Thy Sacred Heart, through the hands of my Mother Mary"—so begins my litany, as I toss into those hands every need I can recall: for my parents and family . . . the people of my parish, especially the lax and fallen-away (particularly right now for old Joe Marron who resists so stubbornly and for Clem Snyder who got married last week in the Lutheran church) . . . for my non-Catholic parishioners too, especially the ones I'm instructing and have instructed . . . for the children of the parish, especially those in public schools . . . for the grace of vocations from this parish, especially for Tommy and Don who are "thinking"—and for the perseverance of those who already have answered Thy call. . . .

For myself, dear Lord, in thanksgiving for the countless graces I have received, in reparation for the sins I have committed, for the grace of final perseverance . . . for Faith, Love, Purity, for zeal in Thy service . . . that I may do Thy will, whether I know that I am doing it or not, whether I want to do it or not: *make* me do Thy will. . . .

For my relatives, friends, and benefactors; for all for whom I ought to pray or have wished to pray; especially for all those to whom I have ever ministered, or for whom I am in any degree responsible—grant that no soul may be lost or may suffer through any fault of mine. (It is here that memory dredges up the discomforting recollections that only the infinite bounty of the Mass can offset: young Eddie, whom I expelled from school when more patience might have saved the pieces; the fallen-away Morellis, who might have been converted by more Christlike kindness when they sought Christian burial for grandpa, and were dismissed so abruptly. When I meditate on Judgment, it isn't my personal sins that make me sweat—Mercy will cover those—it's my pastoral derelictions that make me squirm; I've Justice to deal with there) . . .

For the Pope, for my Ordinary, for the bishop who ordained me and the pastors who guided me and the Sisters who helped form me; for all priests and religious, especially of my own diocese and particularly for the errant—very especially for N. and N. (dear Lord, by what grace am I here and they are gone?); for missionaries, home and foreign—comfort them in their discouragements, fructify their labors by Thy grace. . . .

Yes, it is a long list, and full of detours, images evoked of evil done and good left undone, of individuals in need and souls in distress, of responsibilities shirked and graces wasted. It is well that ten minutes of my morning-prayer time has been reserved for the making of my daily intentions—*aliquantulum* would not be long enough. It is well too that the Mass *is* an inexhaustible torrent; there is so much to pray for, so much. . . .

Et omnium circumstantium. . . . Even as my hands unfold, my burden has lightened and nerves are at ease. With Christ's grace at work on his problems, only a fool would fret.

8:40

THE DOOR of the altar-boys' sacristy slams a farewell, and the so-quickly-emptied church suddenly is still. As I prop elbows on the prie-dieu to begin my thanksgiving, I notice that the candles still send heavenward a thin spiral of smoke. A dying breath of self-immolation, my antic fancy says. *Self-immolation.* There it is again, that ugly word. Ugly as all its brethren are ugly: *penance, self-denial, mortification.* They have been dogging my footsteps these many years, through every page of spiritual reading and every period of meditation. How I have dodged and twisted to escape their relentless pursuit! An ostrich could take lessons from me in purposeful blindness.

"We've a good pastor," my people say—and I am ashamed. Ashamed as I stand beside Katie Connelly at the bed of her just-dead son, and hear her say, "It's God's Will, isn't it, Father?" while she clutches my hand. Ashamed as I stand beside Ed Fetter at his wife's bier, and hear him say, with three little tykes hanging to his pants-legs, "If this is what God wants, we've got to take it, Father." Ashamed as I ride with the Martins to the State Hospital where they are taking their son, and hear the mother say, as she bites her lip, "Well, we've all got to have our cross, Father."

I am a good pastor? Dear God, why shouldn't I be? With my comfortable home, and no mortgage to pay and no sick children to worry about? With social security and old-age security that even a welfare-state couldn't beat? With no clock to punch and no pay to lose if I choose to go to bed with a cold? I've given up a lot, I keep telling myself; yet even my pre-disposed eyes sometimes find it difficult to discern the cross that I must take up, daily, if I would follow Him.

Practiced as I am in evasion, there are times when my defenses are pierced. Turning from the door of a stray sheep hardened in apostasy, I've managed to give a deaf ear to the small voice which whispers, "This kind is cast out by prayer and fasting." But I've not been so successful with, "If any man will come after Me, let him deny himself, and take up his cross daily, and follow Me." That is a barbed shaft against which I still am seeking a counteroffensive. God grant that I may lose the battle, and soon. Because I know I never can win.

In fact I think, I hope, that I've begun to surrender. I love murder mysteries, and I've cut myself down to one a month. I've let the subscriptions to practically all my secular magazines lapse. My radio is seldom turned on. I've made a solemn resolve of obedience to all the rules of liturgy, even wearing a biretta to and from the altar. I haven't been to a Notre Dame football game or a horse race in quite some time. But I've only to turn from that to St. John of the Cross to feel abjectly ridiculous; especially when I remember that I can't do without my before-breakfast cigarette, nor my T-bone steak (rare), nor my sociable highball.

Now what started me on all this? Oh yes, the candles. Well, they're definitely out now, and I'd better be getting on to the *Trium puerorum* if I'm to have hot coffee for breakfast. Of course, it wasn't only the candles. It really was Father Lallemant in last week's meditation. There's one paragraph there that seems to have graven itself uncomfortably deep on my mind: "We spend whole years, and often a whole life, in bargaining whether we shall give ourselves wholly to God. We cannot make up our minds to so complete a sacrifice. We reserve to ourselves many affections, designs, desires, hopes, pretensions, of which we are unwilling to strip ourselves in order to put ourselves in that perfect nudity of spirit which disposes us to be fully possessed by God."

There is a blow that got under my guard, and solidly; a blow that I'm going to feel for a while. A mirror couldn't give me a more perfect picture of myself. I know that my parish could be transformed, if I even started to begin to commence to take the first step toward saintliness. I know that clearly, and yet I am content with prissy little efforts and attempts that hardly are more than subterfuges. Well, the blows have been coming thicker and harder lately. Maybe one of them soon will be the knockout to self-indulgence and sensuality. I hope so. Honestly, dear Lord, I do hope so. It's going to take a miracle to make me what You want me to be, but You've worked miracles before. Please, *please*, don't let me go into eternity still looking the other way. *Trium puerorum*. . . . Now there were *men*.

9:00

LIVING IN THE COUNTRY has its compensations. No morning paper on the table leaves a fellow free to plan his day as he breaks his fast. Today for example I must . . . mmmmm! That first swallow of Annie's potent and fragrant brew makes me breathe a prayer of thanks once again for God's gift of a housekeeper who can make coffee; and who includes among her other charms cleanliness, discretion, cheerfulness, with the crowning grace of complete loyalty. Loyalty—I meditate as I chomp—loyalty is the quality that comes cheapest of all. It is purchased at the price of considerateness, common courtesy indeed. Not that I can take any credit for being considerate, I reflect wryly; it's a natural habit and not a virtue—a habit drilled into me by a wise mother and membership in a family of seven. I still can hear that firm and patient voice, "Leo, take your coat off that chair and hang it up"; "Leo, put that magazine you were reading back on the table"; "Leo, come up here and put these dirty clothes in the hamper where they belong." I remember that I grumbled; but I did it, and a habit was formed—a habit that pays dividends now in the form of a housekeeper who could get more money elsewhere any day that she chose to leave.

Not that I haven't had my moments of reversion. Flashbacks are thrown unbidden on my mental screen: three of us, assistants, gorging on watermelon in the kitchen at St. Alice's, filling the sink with seeds and piling the rinds on the drainboard; the while we discussed, oddly enough, the temperamentalness and general bossiness of house-keepers. There is the picture too of the overturned ash-tray, left lying where it fell ("let her clean it up; that's what she's paid for"). The picture of muddied shoes trailed through the house ("I'm in a hurry, and a little mopping won't hurt her"). There is the picture of a priest's room, bed-clothes trailing across the floor, papers scattered underfoot, books piled precariously on window-sill and radiator. Queer creatures do sometimes wear the rectory apron. But as I look back through my own spotty years, I wonder that more of them aren't permanently demented.

It seems to me—as I bite into my second piece of toast—it seems to me that the difference between a happy priestly home and a mere clerical boarding house is spelled by that one word, "considerateness." It is such a little virtue, and so easily overlooked among the bigger issues. The obvious virtues challenge our effort, but I have known pastors who were chaste and sober and just, yet whose rectories lacked the atmosphere of tranquillity and happiness that an assistant has a right to find in a home that has been thrust upon him. And I have known assist-ants who were pious and zealous and conscientious, yet who have with consistent thoughtlessness made more than one pastor wish he had never left the country.

Come to think about it, a good case could be made for considerateness as an aid to priestly sanctity—considera-tion of pastor for assistants, of assistants for pastor, and of both for the housekeeper. It's a lot easier to be prayerful in an atmosphere of peace and contentment. It is an atmosphere in which even cows are rumored to give more milk. It is an atmosphere which makes poor business for psychiatrists. And it is an atmosphere which so readily and easily can be fashioned. The first ingredient would be a deliberate thoughtfulness for others; there would have to be a hearty disdain for standing on one's "rights" and a cheerful willingness to waive one's prerogatives; to be imposed upon and to carry more than one's share of the burden would have to be expected and accepted as a matter of course. There would have to be actual rivalry in seeing who could be first to grab the dirty end of the stick. Well, maybe the prescription isn't quite so easy to compound as I thought—especially when there is a hold-out in the rectory family, an unreconstructed member who is quite willing to let the others be the do-gooders. But even a hazy sky is better than no sunshine at all.

As I recall my errant brothers whose names no longer appear in the Directory (save them, God, and forgive me!) it is startling to realize in how many cases their trouble began with friction, discontent, resentment, within the walls of what should have been their home. It is so easy for us priests to become self-righteous, and self-righteousness and harmony are so completely antithetic. Father Faber in his *Spiritual Conferences* describes "the censoriousness of a man who has mortified himself into bitterness, because his grace has not been potent enough to overcome his natural incapacity for sweetness." Even more bitingly another writer observes that, "It is almost incredible how some men have narrowed the circle of what they love and esteem, until they have made themselves the one model and type of perfection." Oh yes? Then how about myself as I sit here so smugly self-complacent, sipping my coffee and reforming the world? Maybe I'd better poke a few quotations at myself—like, "God has made man the judge of himself only to condemn himself, and of others only to excuse them." That's from *Sancta Sophia*, and I'd better hang on to it tight. How did I get started on this anyway? Housekeepers, that was it! Maybe some modern Bossuet should write a poem which they could hang in their rooms—"My God, what a life! And it is yours, O Housekeeper to a priest."

9:15

THIS IS the morning that the Master and I pay our monthly visit to old Mrs. Diller, lying helpless with her broken hip. As I blow out the candles and turn from the tabernacle with hand on burse, there comes again that never-failing thrill which accompanies these trips with the Divine Physician. Sliding under the wheel of my waiting Ford, I reflect that in all probability I am theologically attenuated and rankly sentimental, but His presence there on the seat beside me is very real to me. I have forgotten the burse that hangs at my breast. We look out through the car windows together, He and I. "Poor Max Corrigan," I hear myself murmur as we pass the ashes of burned barns, "he'll need a lot of help this year, he and his kids." Almost, out of the corner of my eye, I can see my Passenger nod and smile assent. It's in the bag, I think to myself. Max can quit worrying. I say nothing as we pass the home where a sorrowing grandmother is caring for infant Marie, *pater ignotus;* I say nothing, but there is no mistaking the gentle pity in the Eyes that look out with mine. I swing the wheel sharply as we pass poor foolish Walter, trudging along the road; and my Companion waves with me to the innocent soul in the body of fifty years.

If the trip is long—sometimes we travel seven or eight

miles without a stop—I finger my rosary as He tells me of our Mother. Other times I try to entertain Him with the hymns of my youth, the ones that cause raised eyebrows in proper musical circles. Birds on the fences cock startled heads as, "While ages course along," blasts from the car's open window. But my Guest doesn't object; it's the voice He gave me.

Sometimes we just ride in silence, as He helps me with my problems. It is on these very trips that He has taught me that I am never closer to Him, except in the Mass, than when I go with Him to visit His beloved sick, His own suffering Members. It seems incredible now that there ever was a time when sick-calls were a painful chore, to be made only when I was specifically (and inescapably) called in by the family. It seems unbelievable that I could ever have let other duties—school, meetings, athletics—crowd out this most essential one. Unimaginable as it may seem, that's the way it once was.

Only with the passing years did I recognize the truth that now seems so obvious—that I am with Christ, that I *am* Christ, on these calls. He need not be with me sacramentally. Whether I go to administer Holy Communion, or only to give a priestly blessing and a cheerful word of encouragement, I am conscious of the almost physical nearness of my Master. This indeed, I have discovered, is the charity that covers a multitude of sins. Where once I closed my ears to casual reports of illness and suffering, I have learned now the joy of searching them out. It is He Who has taught me the pleasure of walking in unexpectedly on an illness that was not deemed serious enough to "need" the priest; it is to Him that I humbly refer the grateful surprise that is mirrored in suffering eyes.

Strangely enough, no other duty of the day seems to

suffer from time that has been devoted to the sick. Books of pastoral theology, I reflect, might well feature a chart of priestly obligations, graded as to importance. At the very top, and labeled, *Absolute Must*, would be: ZEAL FOR THE SICK AND AILING. Below that would come such other things as catechizing, sermonizing, organizing.

The pay-off is (as my sporting committeeman is wont to say)—the pay-off is that nothing will win a priest the love of his people, hale and halt alike, so quickly as will the apostolate to the sick. Be he ever so irascible, demanding, cantankerous—everything is forgiven the pastor if his people know that they can count on him to be beside them, a gentle father and a tower of strength, when sickness lays them low. Even a week's bout with the flu is not beneath the notice of the Divine Physician. It was on one of our rides together that He told me to advise my people: "If anyone in the family is sick enough to need the doctor, be sure to let your pastor know."

And how they love, these sufferers, the blessings and the rich and varied prayers which give new meaning to their illness. They sense, if they do not fully understand, the real meaning of the Mystical Body of Christ, as the Church draws upon her vast fund of strength to support and invigorate the weak.

There are other graces, too, that flow from homes of sickness. Just a week ago last Sunday I almost stopped in my tracks at the Communion rail; old Joe Kearns was kneeling there, to receive his Lord for the first time in forty years; my frequent visits to his bed-ridden wife may have been God's vehicle of grace. . . . It was only this morning that Mrs. Vandercook called up to ask if she could begin instructions. The Master is not fussy; He went with me to call on Mrs. Vandercook when she almost lost her last baby.

Well, here we are at Diller's. This muddy old car doesn't look much like a royal chariot, I muse, as we pull up at the kitchen steps. Through the door's glass I can see the candle burning. Mrs. Diller's daughter is waiting for me there—the married daughter, who has started coming to church since Christ started coming to her mother. She sent her children to the Catholic school this year, too, and soon they'll make their first Holy Communion. That will make Mrs. Diller very happy. It will make Him very happy, too. Funny what a broken hip can do.

9:30

SCARCELY have I shucked myself of hat and coat when the door-bell sounds an imperious summons. Through the glass of the door I can see my visitor—a salesman by the looks of him, with a briefcase under his arm. That moment of leisure with my first pipeful of the morning will have to be postponed. There comes that twinge of impatience, always in evidence when God's Will collides with mine. Why do there *have* to be salesmen—why can't they let us do our ordering by phone or by mail? But with my hand on the doorknob, the twinge is subdued. It is a long time since I learned my lesson of courtesy to all comers, but the years have not dimmed that lesson's effect. . . .

He was a little fellow, on the rotund side, and fire-extinguishers was his line. I didn't want any fire-extinguishers, and I did want to get away for my appointment—an important one with three other priests and a golf ball. I told him quite civilly that I wasn't interested, but he was the pesky kind: he was sure I never had seen anything quite like his product; couldn't he come in and show it to me? Father Vicinus had bought three of them and thought they were wonderful. It would only take a minute—

He was shot down in mid-flight. If he'd had any sense

he'd have seen me poised for the attack: "Listen, didn't you hear me say I wasn't interested? I don't want any, so quit wasting your time and mine. Beat it, will you?" Only I'm afraid maybe it sounded worse than that. He turned away as the door slammed, and I watched him down the steps. It was then that I noticed the neat little patch on the back of his top-coat, and the run-down heels, and the overdue haircut. It was the little patch that got me—that and the grace of God, being as I'm not given by nature to generous impulses. So I shrugged off the golf date (it looked like rain anyway) and called him back and tried to give a reasonable facsimile of a gentleman by my apology. We sat down and he showed me his wares and I told him what we had and he agreed we were pretty well covered.

Then we visited, over pipe and cigarette. He lived in a neighboring state, with his wife and four youngsters. His wife was a Catholic, and he himself was taking instructions, almost ready for baptism. (How I squirmed at that! He was a catechumen, and I, a priest, had ordered him off the premises!). We parted friends, he with a rosary which I somewhat sheepishly slipped into his hand. It was good to see him turn back at the foot of the steps, and smile. It *was* starting to drizzle. I decided to go over to the school; the children hadn't seen me in a week.

Well, it was easier after that to suffer the plague of phone and doorbell. Whenever my natural snappishness strained at the leash, I had only to conjure a vision of a wifely patch on the back of a coat. Candle salesmen, wine salesmen, vestment agents and soap peddlers—I turn up the corners of my mouth as I open the door for each, and invite them in before I ask their business. My time is God's time, and God's time is all for souls. This man with the briefcase may be some other pastor's good parishioner, using part of his hard-earned commissions to support the Church and to send his kids to the parish school; this fellow with the order-book sticking out of his pocket may be another priest's convert, or he may be the wrong side of a mixed marriage; even this glib lad with the Masonic emblem is one of the lot of us for whom Christ died. Any one of them, or all of them, may be influenced for life by the impression they carry away of me, a man of God. So it's, "Come in. Sorry I don't need any, but sit down a minute, anyway, and rest yourself a bit." Courtesy is so *cheap*, so easy.

So easy? Maybe that's over-simplifying a bit. I can't honestly ever be too sure of myself, whether it's a stubborn salesman, or a pestiferous parent, or a child with a rosary to bless. I still find myself having to apologize to someone, at least twice or thrice a year. It's in periods of stress and strain that courtesy costs the most. School-opening time, Holy Week, the last week of Advent—such as these are the danger spots. And how it hurts to apologize, especially when I know that I am right and the other party is wrong, as, strangely enough, always seems to be the case. But the other party isn't a priest; the other party isn't the one expected to set the good example. And the other party doesn't need the discipline nor the penance of apologizing half as much as I.

It's funny, too, what strong friendships can be born of an apology. Last Christmas my nicest gifts came from two persons to whom I've made myself apologize in times past. Not that I'd recommend apology as a career. But certainly there's many a wound in the Mystical Body that could so easily have been healed by a word of honest regret; or better still, wounds that never need have happened if patience had been at her post.

My hand still is on the doorknob. It has taken me a long time to open the door, and my friend on the other side is reaching doubtfully for the bell again. So up, up with the corners of the mouth. He's earning his living the hard way, and maybe he's got a patch on the back of his coat.

9:45

As I stand outside the door of the eighth-grade room, it is, as always, with a sense of inadequacy that I await the sound of the bell which will signal the beginning of the religion period. Through the door's glass I can see forty-odd heads turned toward Sister as she explains square-root at the blackboard. Forty-odd heads which ought to know God better, forty-odd hearts which ought to love Him more. In a moment I shall go in for my weekly stint, and forty-odd voices will chant, "Good morning, Father," and forty-odd pairs of eyes will look at me expectantly; glad for the break in the monotony, not really caring much what I have to say.

Last week they were beginning their unit on the Church, and I talked about the Mystical Body. Since then they have been learning about the martyrs, so today I shall talk to them about the power of good example. With pointed questions I shall draw them on in the hope that they themselves may find the objective and enjoy the thrill of discovery. But I shall leave the room as I entered it, with a feeling of frustration that is saved from despair only by a consciousness of the potency of God's grace.

Forty-odd impressionable minds, forty-odd characters in the formative stage, every one a potential saint or sinner. Dick there might easily go to the seminary and become an exemplary priest, or he might just as easily become a drunken bum like his Uncle George. Louise there—I can easily see her as the lovely Catholic mother of half a dozen kids, yet I know she may end up a selfish wench married to a divorced man. What will spell the difference, and how much of the responsibility will be mine?

Perhaps the heavy-heartedness is exaggerated today; Mrs. Borden's visit still is too fresh in my mind. She came in last night to tell me about her daughter Eileen, married yesterday by a Methodist minister to a man who doesn't like priests. "And here's the medal she won right here in school, Father, the medal for Christian Doctrine." The poor soul was clutching it in her hand as though to prove that the whole thing was a mistake, a bad dream that would go away. Yes, I remember Eileen; she could always be counted on for the answer when everyone else was stymied.

Now where, *where* is the responsibility for the likes of Eileen, the too-numerous likes of Eileen? They spend eight, twelve, even sixteen years in the shadow of the altar, and then turn out to be spiritual tramps. Maybe the curriculum can take part of the rap: so many expertly designed courses that teach all the answers, but not how to live. The children use their missals at Mass with mechanical perfection, but have no vision of themselves as a part of the Bread that is being offered. (Some morning I should like to say Mass in the classroom, with just a table, a large one, for an altar, with the children gathered around and all receiving Communion. And then after Mass they would spread the table with the food they had brought for breakfast, and share their food together. Impractical of course, but what a lasting object-lesson it could be!)

But it's not for me to be belaboring the curriculum. I've not got enough credits in education to set myself up as an authority there. Much less shall I make scapegoats of the Sisters. Poor souls, with five and six subjects to prepare for each day, they do well to master the text itself, without being expected to give it the flesh and flush of life.

Well, if I skip the text and skip the teachers, that brings me right smack up against me! After all, I *am* the shepherd; they *are* my lambs. I may as well face it: when one of my flock goes wrong, there's something of me in the failure. When they crack under pressure, it isn't lack of knowledge that's responsible, it's lack of love. And love is not something that's learned out of books or at a blackboard. It isn't learned at all, it's imparted. It is a fire that is ignited by contact. I should never enter a classroom reluctantly, hesitantly, if my heart were bursting, as it ought to be, with love for Jesus Christ. I should never need to wonder what to say as I faced His little ones, if the pressure in my own heart were straining for escape.

How the Mass would stand out in the fourth dimension of Love! How the concept of the Mystical Body would rise living and breathing from the limbo of sterile imagery! How the distasteful duties of prayer and sacrifice would become, instead, challenges to divine adventure. Yes, it could happen here, it could happen now. All it takes is a holy priest, a saintly pastor. "And listen, Father T"—it's my Guardian Angel talking, and there are times I could gladly choke him—"listen now! Quit dodging the issue. Quit trying to whistle yourself by the cemetery. *Do* something about it, *right now!*"

The bell sets up its clamor, and forty-odd pairs of eyes swing from Sister to the door. Here comes mediocrity to teach perfection. I've got the picture now: a wavering and uncertain finger pointing to dim heights. I've got to clear my vision, and that bit of ocular therapy will have to begin at the knees.

10:00

PEDAGOGY has traveled far since my own boyhood. Today the eighth-graders are having a "socialized recitation." Joey is on his feet telling us about St. Lawrence, while all around the room others are rising and poising to supply the details that Joey will forget. One thing he doesn't forget: "Turn me over"—Joey is quoting St. Lawrence—"turn me over, I think I'm done on that side now." The kids appreciate the humor of the sizzling Saint, and there is a general chuckle as they look to see if I am enjoying it, too. I grin back, even as I wish that I had St. Lawrence's gift for discounting my own self-importance. There, I reflect, is a natural patron for moments of discouragement. Discouragement inevitably means that I am taking myself too seriously; always it accompanies that mood in which I seem to feel that I must save the world single-handed. . . .

A parishioner calls to tell me of a recently arrived neighboring couple who are married out of the Church. Maybe if I could call on them. . . ? The name and address go down on the desk pad, to be added to six similar ones awaiting attention. I sigh as I turn back to the task of drafting a raffle ticket for our forthcoming picnic. "Is this what I was ordained for?" I ask myself. Fifty per cent of my working hours spent at a desk, raising money, paying bills, listening to salesmen, writing letters, planning with contractors, supervising repairs, cranking a mimeograph and filling out forms? Nine-tenths of it a layman could do, and meanwhile there are souls to be saved on every side of me. Ernie Stein, for example. I read in last night's paper that he was married Saturday in the Baptist church. It's just a year and a half since I baptized Ernie, a promising convert. He broke up with his Catholic girl friend shortly after. Now maybe if I'd followed him up a bit, kept in closer touch with him. . . ?

Right here is a good spot for St. Lawrence to step in: "Listen, my flurried friend," he says, "I may be only a deacon, but let me tell you a few things. What you're doing has to be done. Maybe a layman *could* do it, but just the same, if you don't do it, it won't get done. These desk jobs you moan about are part of your work, dedicated and made fruitful in your morning offering. Give God credit for a little sense. He knows how much time you've got, and He's made His plans accordingly. After all, two cents worth of His grace can accomplish more than two gallons of your sweat; you believe that, don't you?"

By this time St. Lawrence has settled himself, with one foot on a chair, for what I can see is going to be a good lecture. "Just remember," he says, "that God's been in this business of saving souls a lot longer than you have. He's not asleep on the job, even when you seem to be piddling away your time running a movie projector for the Holy Name Society. The trouble with you, Father" —St. Lawrence wags his finger within an inch of my nose —"the trouble with you is that you're not so much interested in souls being saved as you are in *seeing* them saved; you want to be able to check them off as definitely present and accounted for. I can't reveal any secrets, but you may be surprised some day to find how many Protestants you prayed into Heaven without ever being able to include them in your annual report. Don't think that God is limited by the figures in the Catholic Directory."

My visitor pauses, but not for long: "Look at Father Harrumph," he admonishes, "he thought the job was too big for him, so he took to alcohol; and what good is he doing anyone now, in a sanitarium? Then there's Father Hustle, a chronic cardiac case, and Father Hurry with a nice set of ulcers; each thought that the world would go to pot if he didn't carry it personally on his shoulders. Now wait a minute"—Lawrence raises his hand to check my objection—"don't tell me about the saints who burned themselves out laboring for souls. When you're a saint I'll be willing to come back and discuss that with you. As soon as you start spending the whole night in prayer before the Tabernacle. . . . By the way"—Lawrence interrupts himself—"did you ever stop to think how much more fruitful your time would be if you did spend more of it in prayer, and less in running circles around yourself? Try that for a change. There's time enough to worry when a golf match means more to you than a convert instruction, or an all-night poker game more than your health.

"Well," Lawrence grins as he takes his foot off the chair, "I've been pretty serious, considering my reputation for a sense of humor. But just the same, don't forget what Marshal Foch said to his flatterers, 'Gentlemen, God could have done as much with a broken broom-handle.' There are far more worried priests than there are lazy priests, and I don't know but what the worriers dishonor God the more. . . ."

(45)

Eager snapping fingers recall me with a start. Joey has finished his recitation. As I clear my throat and dispel my reverie, I make a quick resolution: next time the appointment book is loaded and the day seems too short, instead of reaching for the baking soda, I'll just say, "St. Lawrence, pray for me!"

10:15

THE MORNING'S STINT in school completed, I dawdle my way back to the rectory, still thinking about the children. They are a responsibility that weighs heavily. "Give me the child, and you can have the man." Hitler made it work—almost; the Commies seem to make it work; but do we? I'm not too sure. For a good many years now I've been talking glibly, like everyone else, about the children being our hope for the future. Yet the future, when it arrives, seems suspiciously like the past. And no one in all the wide world has such a chance at the children as do we priests.

There I go again, taking refuge in the crowd; talking about "we" and "us" when I should be saying "I" and "me." The only part of the world I'm going to have to answer for is right here within the boundaries of old St. Pat's. So far as I am concerned, the only youngsters in the world to be fashioned and formed are the kids in the little brick school on Exeter Road. Well, what am I doing to make them just a little bit better than their mothers and fathers? Not that their mothers and fathers aren't good enough, in an inoffensive sort of way. But a stranger would have a hard time distinguishing them from the mothers and fathers who got their start at the Lutheran school down by Sandy Creek, or from the mothers and fathers who learned their Bible lessons from old Reverend Merrill at the Methodist church-house. Week-days, they all seem cut to a pattern. They enjoy the same gossip, the same beer-gardens, the same trivialities.

If their offspring are going to be any different, I'm the one who will have to give them the boost, under God. It isn't that I don't know what the kids need. I'm quite sure that the doctrine of the Mystical Body, with its social implications for seven-day-week living, is the very dynamite they're waiting for, if only somebody—I mean if I could light the fuse. The trouble is, indoctrinating them in the truth of the Mystical Body, keyed to their level, would mean a powerful lot of work; a lot of study and meditation on my part. Shucks, the tract wasn't even in Tanquerey when I went to the seminary. I'd have to read the Encyclical, *Mystici Corporis*, and maybe two or three good books besides.

And it wouldn't end there. The Mystical Body would lead logically to the Liturgy. I'd feel that I had to read those bound volumes of the *Proceedings of the Liturgical Weeks* which have been gathering dust on my shelves, and maybe Pius Parsch and Abbot Marmion and a few others. There'd be results, of course. With the Mass come alive and the sacraments loved, the front pews might fill up first on Sundays; there might even be the lovely sound of many feet coming up the aisle on week days.

But I'm so *busy*. There isn't time for so much study and so much thinking; above all for so much thinking. But wait; let me be honest if nothing else. How about adding up the hours I spend skimming through the *Saturday Evening Post*, paging through *Life*, looking at the cartoons in *Collier's*, reading at least the "important" articles in *Reader's Digest*, not to mention my cover-to-cover consumption of *Time?* I tell myself that I must be well informed and abreast of the world, but in my lucid moments I have to admit that ninety per cent of what I read is hog-wash, forgotten within a week. It isn't information that I'm seeking, but escape; escape from the awful labor of thinking. All my so-called information doesn't even make for good conversation. Someone asks me if I've read such-and-such an article in the *Digest*, and I say, "Yes," and he says, "Oh," and that ends the discussion. If I say, "No, what's it about?" at once I'm a friend to him who is so anxious to tell me.

All right, I'll let my subscriptions expire. (As I tick them off on my fingers, I reflect that CARE can well use the money I'll save.) This next school year I'll start giving an hour religiously—in more ways than one—to the two upper grades. I'll study and master and teach the Mystical Body until those kids can see It move and breathe, and themselves a part of It. I'll make myself know the Liturgy as I should have known it years ago—its meaning and its power and its beauty. I'll get to love it with a love that I can pass on to the youngsters, until they'll be jumping in their seats with eagerness for it; fairly seeing the characters of baptism and confirmation shining through their ribs; praying the Mass and singing the Mass to make the windows rattle. I'll start off a generation that will stand out in this community as twenty-four-hour-a-day Christians. I'll . . .

I mean, I hope I will. But it would be so much easier to follow beaten paths. Why stick my neck out? After all, what the Ordinary requires and what the Confraternity Director imposes, should be good enough for me. The Sisters can teach the children better than I can; they're trained for it. Besides, I'll probably get changed about the time I'm nicely started . . . or else the whole thing will flop . . . or else . . . Well, doggone it, I can *try*. *Deus me confirmet*.

10:30

As I SETTLE down to pray the Little Hours, I reflect how appropriate is the jocose reference to one's Breviary as, "my wife." There is the honeymoon period, immediately after sub-deaconship, when the *ordinatus* and his breviary are ostentatiously inseparable, when there is thrill and pride in announcing, "I have to say my Office now." Then comes the priesthood and the coldly realistic years when midnight gallops down the stretch to a photo-finish with the *Sacrosanctae;* when the *Opus Dei* becomes the *Onus Diei,* and one secretly wishes that those people in Rome had to do an American priest's work for just a week or so. Then come the mellow years, as one's hair turns gray; the years when that dominating partner in black and gold becomes a comfortable, even a beloved companion; when there is real affection in the kiss-on-leather that accompanies one's rise from creaky knees. Finally comes the day when Father can read no more; his Breviary is there by the bed, the silent comforter of his weakening hours. And when Father has been laid to rest, no widow's weeds are *half* so poignant as the greasy pages and the shabby cover of the Book he has left behind.

Those middle years were the hard ones, I recall as I stoop to recover my marker. They were hard because I made them hard. They were hard because I adhered to the common heresy of work before prayer, and because mine was the natural disorder of youth. Not for me was a rule of life, with a time set aside for essentials. The hours poured out of my day like money from a wastrel's hand; I did not reckon values, so long as I could spend. There was the further difficulty of lingual inadequacy. Parish high school and college Lit course had left me severely handicapped in the tongue of Cicero and Augustine—a handicap that still leaves me trembling whenever a youngster approaches me with his Latin book to ask, "Father, what does this sentence mean?"

But the passage of time brought, if not wisdom, at least adjustment. There was the assurance of a wise retreat-master that literal understanding was not necessary; the reminder that in reciting the Divine Office I was a mouthpiece of the Mystical Body, and that the *ecclesia orans* was praising God through me, regardless of my own comprehension. He reminded me, too, of the merit of obedience, a merit that increases with the distastefulness and the difficulty of the task performed. Little by little then, my resentment at having to pray in an alien tongue decreased. It was a resentment that died completely when I had occasion to recite the Office in English at Sodality and Catholic Action meetings. Awkward English phrases which made me wince, and expressions which in English sounded ridiculous and invited to snickers—these effected my final conversion. There came the incredible day when I, the Latin-hater, was glad that my Breviary was in Latin.

As I riffle the pages of *Pars Aestiva*, I remember that there were other things which helped to remove the Divine Office from my list of adversaries. There was the stubbornly resisted but eventual consciousness that certain things are incompatible with prayer—the radio, for example. It was easy to see that it was hardly less than sinful to pretend to pray while a ball-game or a newscast blocked all true communication with Heaven. But for a long time I did fancy that soft music made a harmless background for my orisons; until I got my psychology straight and realized that even soft music exacts a modicum of attention which is that much less for God.

Then there were the sociable evenings with my own family or at another rectory, when I would drop out of the conversation or the card game and go into the next room to finish my Office. The voices, the jokes and the laughter still came clearly to my ears, so I wasn't really missing anything. Not anything except the merits of honest prayer. When some undeserved grace brought that fact home to me, I saw that there must be a time set aside for the Office; a time with which nothing but genuine emergencies could be allowed to conflict; a time that would see today's Office, at least, completed before evening. So now it is Prime before Mass, Little Hours at ten-thirty or at least before lunch, Vespers and Compline after lunch, and Matins and Lauds before dinner if I'm lucky. There are times when circumstances require adjustments, but there has to be a rule before there can be exceptions.

Well, this reminiscing isn't getting Little Hours said. I open the Book determinedly. Today is one of those beautiful Spring days when it's good just to be alive. I'll watch for verses that will express that mood—*Exsultate, justi, in Domino*. Some days (they should be more frequent) my mood is penitential; then it is for such phrases as, *Infirmata est in paupertate virtus mea*, that I watch.

Another day I'll be grateful; maybe a big sinner back or (let's be honest) a big stipend in. Then such lines as, *Ego autem in Domino speravi: exsultabo et laetabor in misericordia tua*, will hold special meaning for me. A silly thing, maybe, saying one's Office according to mood. But there is one thing the years haven't brought, and that is an increase in my knowledge of Latin. Making my Breviary a part of today's mental outlook fixes attention and gives vitality to the prayer, as I watch for a word here, a sentence there, that will express how I feel *now*.

Well, Lord, here I come; illiterate Leo speaking for the Church Universal. It's amazing how easily satisfied you are, O Lord. Perhaps some soul in Russia will be saved, perhaps some soul in my own parish will be spared a temptation, because of what I am about to do. *In nomine Patris, et Filii, et Spiritus Sancti. . . .*

10:45

Little hours finished, my hand reaches out for a cigarette, with a practiced motion that is almost instinctive. No wonder; it is a motion that is repeated thirty times or more in every twenty-four hours. And just as many times a day, including now, my conscience gives its all-too-familiar prick. Here we go again, I wryly reflect—match poised in hand—here we go again, my conscience and I, around and around in the same old circle. *Conscience:* Why don't you quit smoking? *Myself:* I suppose I should. *Conscience:* Of course you should; it's the one thing in your life that you're really attached to. How can you talk about mortification while you smoke a pack and a half a day? *Self:* But I enjoy smoking! And you know yourself that Doc Fitzgerald said it wasn't hurting my health any. Besides, I do remember now and then to thank God for the pleasure I'm getting from it; doesn't that make it all right? *Conscience:* Of course not. It seems a sin to enjoy anything just for the pleasure you get out of it. Any action that hasn't got a supernatural end is vitiated by that very fact.

Self: You mean to say that it's wrong for me to love to see the setting sun come slanting across the cornfield, there outside my study window? Wrong to enjoy the smell of the lilacs in the spring or the smell of burning leaves in the autumn? Wrong to. . . . *Conscience:* Whoa, wait a minute; we're talking about smoking. Can you name me one canonized saint who smoked? *Self:* Well now, if it's "ad hominem" arguments you want, let me ask whether you can name a saint who was denied canonization because he smoked, or chewed, or snuffed? And anyway, I thought we were talking about sin, rather than sanctity. If you put it on the basis of sanctity, maybe we could get together. Just show me where it's sinful for me to smoke; I'll quit in a minute.

Conscience: Well, maybe not sinful, but you'd be a better man if you did quit, right now. *Self:* No, not right now. Know what would happen if I quit smoking right now? I'd be proud as the devil of my will power; I'd have a fine scorn—concealed maybe—for my weaker brethren who still smoked; I'd be so busy preening myself that I'd forget all the other more important mortifications that I should be working on. *Conscience:* More important? What, for example?

Self: Now don't tell me, my friend, that you don't know that interior mortification is more important than exterior. Take Saturday night, for instance; nine o'clock, and confession time officially is ended. If I had the zeal I should, I'd not be hurrying to lock the church door before a late-comer arrives to detain me. If I were mortified interiorly, I'd be reluctant to lock the door—I'd be peering down the road to see if another prodigal might be coming. Or take any day in the office, when I've got plans of my own, and someone comes in on some picayune business and wants to sit and talk. If I were mortified interiorly, I'd see that person as God's Will, and not be in such a lather to get rid of him. Or take last Sunday afternoon, when I was getting set for a nice rest, and heard that old Mrs. Ebers needed someone to drive her forty miles to see her husband in the hospital. If I were mortified interiorly, I shouldn't have had to argue with myself for fifteen minutes before going to the phone and volunteering to drive her. There are a few examples of what I mean by more important mortifications. I could quit smoking, and still be mighty selfish, and thoughtless, and cantankerous. Abstinence from nicotine wouldn't profit me half as much as another thirty minutes a day spent in prayer. If I loved God enough. . . .

Conscience: Yes, I can see what you're getting at. If you loved God enough, mortification would come easy. Heroic self-denial is the result of goodness, rather than the cause. If you can advance in the love of God, your self-attachments will shed themselves like the peeling of an onion, layer by layer until there's nothing left. You figure that the day might even come when it will seem natural and inevitable to quit smoking—a day when you'll find more happiness in giving it up than in clinging to the habit. In other words, progress in virtue has got to be by more fundamental means than mortification merely for mortification's sake. Well, maybe I'd better call this argument a draw, and change my line of attack. How long do you think it's going to take you to quit smoking, your way?

Self: Only God can tell. Sometimes I think even He must get discouraged trying to temper me so that I'll hold an edge. Maybe there just isn't enough carbon in the steel. But keep after me, Conscience; if we work this out at all, it will have to be with your help. Miracles of grace do happen, and the day may come when I'll actually feel joy in sprinkling ashes on my food and in sleeping on a board. Meanwhile, with due thanks to God and respect for the virtue of temperance, I'll continue to enjoy a good meal. In the cause of fraternity and with respect to the virtue of sobriety, I'll continue to take a highball with my brethren before a clerical dinner. It seems safe doctrine to say that all that God has done is good; surely the emotion of innocent pleasure is the work of His Hands, and cannot be classed as a vitiating principle? So until. . . .

Conscience: Look out! That match is burning your fingers. Go ahead and light up and quit philosophizing. I only hope you're not rationalizing. Anyway, I've got work to do; I've got to get busy sharpening up another prod.

11:00

JOE HEIMS (he works the afternoon shift) is due for his semi-weekly instruction. As I doodle on my desk pad while waiting for him, the memory of Joe's first visit comes back to me. It was hesitantly that he told me that he wanted to become a Catholic. His mother had been a Catholic, but he himself never had been baptized. He felt that it was time now that he should be.

As I talked with him casually, trying to set him at ease, I found that he lived several miles away—in another parish, really. How then had he happened to come here? "Well," Joe explained, "I've been wanting to talk to a priest for quite a while, but I guess I was kind of scared. Here a couple of days ago when I was in Charlie Ort's gas station, Charlie was telling me what an easy guy you are to talk to. Charlie says you never did bawl anybody out. So I just decided I'd come and see you." I blinked my eyes with a quick but fervent prayer of thanks that Charlie doesn't know me as well as he thinks he does. Then Joe and I went on from there.

Now, as I wait, I ruminate again on the bigness of a little kindness. It's as tiny a seed as the biblical mustard, and its branches spread just as wide. More and more with the passing years, as I flounder about in the net of routine and detail, my youthful dreams of real missionary work fade fainter in the distance. As it becomes progressively less possible to go out to others, I take refuge in the hope that I may be a priest to whom those others, impelled by God's grace, may fearlessly and confidently come. And so I resolve again to pray harder for the virtue of kindness, and to be more vigilant against failure.

Because it is so easy to fail. It is so easy to visit my early morning grouch upon a hapless altar boy; so easy to scold the children who run across the lawn and disturb my rest with their shouts beneath my window. It is so easy to be abrupt when someone phones at an unreasonable hour to ask a silly question that was answered in last Sunday's announcements; so easy to excoriate a gossiping parishioner, when I hear that she has publicly questioned my infallibility. It is so easy to be incensed at the Sodality chairman whose youthful irresponsibility has brought failure to a pet project; so easy to put in his place the stubborn parish committeeman who is so arrogant in his ignorance.

These things are easy. But it is so hard to smile and be accommodating when I've got a splitting headache and would like a little sympathy; so hard to be tranquil when lax parents ask for Baptism at a special hour for a baby that should have been brought a month ago; so hard to say, "yes," when invited to a marriage feast, with a good book left unread at home; so hard to. . . . But what's the need of going on? It's so doggone hard not to be human; so hard to be Christlike.

And so necessary, too. Necessary, that is, if a fellow is going to face Judgment in any spirit of hopefulness. Looking back over twenty-odd years of priesthood, I can't recall a single fallen-away who said he left the church because the pastor was a drunkard or a libertine.

But on all my fingers and all my toes I cannot count the ex-Catholics who "Had a fight with the priest," "Had an argument with Father Griper"—"The pastor told me to get out and stay out," "The priest told me I was no good," and so on, through all the changes that are so familiar to any parish visitator. In many cases mere alibis, of course. Yet it remains evident that the priest who succumbs to the weaknesses of the flesh, even to the point of apostasy, does not damage the credentials of Christ's Church one-tenth as much as the priest who is unkind.

It would be wonderful, I reflect, if we priests as a class were known as "The kindest men in the world"! The day is gone when the clergy were looked upon as the world's most learned body. In an age of materialism and unbelief we are denied credit for being the most continent group in the world. Our own compromises with secularism make it doubtful whether we could claim the world's championship for asceticism. But kindness—gosh, that should be easy! It should be, except that a thing like that is never done by a group; it's done by the individuals. By me, for example, the least common denominator. It's time I took stock of myself and started a program of giving—giving *myself*.

As I put eyebrows on the freakish face my doodling pencil has sketched, the memory of Father Felix's funeral pops into mind. It was just last week that I went to his funeral. As I walked down the aisle ahead of his body, I noticed the moist eyes and the red noses in almost every pew—and it wasn't colds the people had; they were crying. Because I knew Father Felix, I could almost read their sorrowing minds: "He was such a *kind* man." I'd never thought about it before, but I realized then that I'd been to many a priest's funeral where a dry-eyed congregation watched the corpse wheeled out. It seemed a horrible picture when it first struck me: a priest's own children-in-Christ, staring impassively as their father is buried.

Will they cry at my funeral, I wonder, as I tear off the scribbled sheet and toss it into the basket? Not that there'd be any particular pleasure for me in the thought of weeping faces. But the tears might be an earnest, to a just Judge, of a mercy deserved because of mercy given. What a wonderful tribute it would be to any priest, if on his gravestone it could be graven, without fear of contradiction: "He was kind"!

There goes the doorbell. Joe is here.

11:45

As I STEP into the sacristy for the quarter-hour interlude which I have come to find so welcome, I regret, for the hundredth time, that I have been such an empiricist in matters spiritual. Always I have to learn the hard way. Despite seminary directors and ascetic theologians, I had to discover for myself that one must meditate, or perish. It took me even longer to admit the necessity of the particular examen. That was an exercise I considered as being reserved to nuns and seminarians, with no place in the life of a busy priest. But gradually it was impressed upon me that meditation alone wasn't the whole answer. Good resolutions faded too rapidly. I could feel so otherworldly at 7:00 A. M. and so this-worldly at 7:00 P. M. It was quite evident that my spiritual efforts suffered from the same defect as my bowling—lack of follow-through.

While my knees squirm themselves into a comfortable stance upon the altar-step, I marvel again at the power of God's grace, that can penetrate a skull as thick and as stubborn as mine. I did undertake, eventually, to make an effort at daily examen. It was an effort that escaped failure and abandonment by a very narrow margin—by a margin that perhaps only seemed narrow, since God's grace was the margin.

Two great difficulties presented themselves at the start.

The first difficulty, not too readily recognized, was my own smugness and self-satisfaction. Fifteen minutes seemed ridiculously long for this scrutiny. Strangely enough, I could pass an hour, easily, ruminating on my good points, my supposed talents and achievements. But for the life of me I couldn't find enough defects to occupy a quarter-hour of thought. Oh, not that I claimed to be a saint; but I did feel that I was running a pretty good average. Even now I can feel my face getting warm with merited shame as I recall that I sometimes used to say the rosary during examen time, because "there wasn't anything special to think about"!

Lucky for me that I stayed with it long enough, until the steam began to clear away from the mirror, and I began to see what I really looked like. I realize now why, for so long, I tried to duck particular examen: old man Ego had a presentiment and a dread of the exposure that would result. It isn't pleasant to be caught in a lie, even once. But this stern and merciless mentor called Examen is constantly surprising me in my comfortable self-deceptions.

That was *one* obstacle to establishing this fifteen-minute check-up as a daily habit. The second difficulty was posed by the old and specious shibboleth, "too busy." Whatever I might be doing in the pre-luncheon period— whether making a parochial visit, working at my desk, or talking to a caller—it always seemed to carry me right up to lunch-time. The Angelus would ring, and where was the time for an examen? Well, that difficulty resolved itself when it occurred to me (thank you for the grace, dear Lord) that all I had to do was to move lunch-time ahead by fifteen minutes, and then spend that fifteen minutes in church before going to the table. So simple and so easy! Now my morning's work is planned to terminate, not at twelve, but at eleven forty-five. It is surprising to see how willingly the most persistent caller departs when I say, "I have to go over to church now"; he leaves with less offense, I am sure, than if I had excused myself for lunch.

"Too busy!" There is an escape-mechanism that I still haven't succeeded in exorcising completely. Again and again I have to make it the burden of my examen. Too busy to discharge my first, my *only* obligation, which is to sanctify myself? Can my people suffer because I give time to becoming a better priest? I'm up to my neck in meetings, and plans, and activities. Every night the lights burn in the parish hall. I've organized everyone in the parish except the cats and dogs. I don't have any *time* for myself. Anyone can see how devoted I am to my people, how completely I give myself to them!

Then I think of the Curé of Ars; and "pfutt" goes the barricade I have so feverishly erected against the awful labor of sanctifying myself. How many Boy Scouts and Campfire Girls did the Curé of Ars have? How many softball teams and euchre tournaments and Ushers Clubs? Maybe if I'd just settle down to being a really good priest, a man of prayer and love and sacrifice (they follow in that order), then maybe my confessional would be busy and the communion rail would be crowded without a lot of tub-thumping and endless mimeographing. Not that parish activities won't still have their importance. But I'll see them in their proper perspective, instead of letting the frame grow bigger than the picture.

So I shall build me some fences: fences around meditation-time, and examen-time, and spiritual reading-time. And on those fences I'll plaster big "No Trespassing" signs, just as I do on my meal-time and sleeping-time. Before I try following Paul's example by being all things to all men, I'll first of all try following his example by letting Christ live in me and me in Christ. I have an idea that maybe I've had the sequence wrong.

Oh oh! Here it is three minutes to twelve and I haven't even started my examen, haven't even said the "Come Holy Ghost"! But maybe the time hasn't been wasted. I've been over all this before, but repetition won't hurt; it's an awful thick skull, an *awful* thick skull.

12:00

THE FIRST STROKES of the Angelus sound the end of today's abbreviated examen. Abbreviated or not, I have been able to give myself an uncomfortable minute or two. *Custos oculorum* is the present point for self-scrutiny, a point that I took merely as a formality, quite confident that I should make short work of a matter that touched me so little. But my confidence has weakened considerably. This examen business has such an uncanny facility for uncovering pebbles and showing them to be good-sized stones. I hadn't thought of it before, but now I must admit that even *my* eyes, if not wary, can be trapped by the "cheese-cake" of the secular press, by the shamelessness of a pagan world. Not to mention . . . well, not to mention a lot of things. A lot of things that we might joke about (and do joke about), which don't seem nearly so funny when one is kneeling before the Tabernacle at noon.

No doubt about it, I've given myself food for rumination for a few more examens. *Custos oculorum* will lead to other things. Because the human mind (my mind anyway) can be such a devious deceiver. It can so blandly square the circle, so slyly reconcile contradictory theory and practice. It can give comforting assurance of resistance, when any honest jury would say that reistance came much too late. It will magnify *fragilitas humana* until there is no sin except the dereliction be consummated. Even then it will make a last ditch stand, and plead inadvertence. Driven to the wall, there still is no honorable surrender; it will quibble to the last, and confess, "As God sees me guilty," when it should be saying, "Because God knows I *am* guilty."

I wonder if there are many others like it, this cozening mind of mine? It can be so desperately ashamed—more ashamed than sorry—when failure exposes its weakness; it can be so arrogantly confident that next time it will be a tower of strength. So long as alibis endure, it will evade an honest facing of the facts, such as meditation and examen might induce. "Too busy," and "Tomorrow," will keep the blinders on. An earnest half-hour on my knees might expose, for what it really is, that very evident occasion of sin which I've dodged acknowledging for so long; even fifteen minutes in a quiet church might show me how often I've gone looking for trouble, whistling as though I didn't know that I was in enemy territory.

So many things seem to change complexion by the light of the sanctuary lamp. The so-called "intellectual point," for example, that was supposed to be a magic detergent that would whiten any story; examined here, it doesn't seem quite adequate to offset the scandal given, the tender consciences wounded, the lowered moral tone of teller and listener. I think of the priests I admire most, the ones I'd like to have by my bedside as I die; and I realize that they are the ones whose speech is as clean and sweet today as it was before they ever cracked a moral theology text.

It is now that I wince as I recall so many conferences

on the "holy virtue," which I sat through smugly complacent while the retreat master warned of dangers from the opposite sex. So secure did I feel from dangers without, that I gave no thought (nor did the retreat master, seemingly) to how vulnerable I was from within.

It is now, too, that I recall my all-but-impatient advice to stumbling penitents—prayer, vigilance, avoidance of occasion, quick recourse to Confession—and understand, with something of a shock, how often I have failed to take my own advice. I can see now, as I could not see before, that others will be stronger, if I am less weak; that the flock will be less deviant if the shepherd is more single-eyed.

Grace! That is the golden word! All my self-reproach cannot obscure the fact that God's grace is more than a match even for such a skillful fraud as I have been. "To him who does what in him lies, God's grace will not be wanting," is the stout life-line that becomes visible in this moment of compunction. I know that I must grasp quickly. The time for grace is always NOW. The Prodigal Son didn't dilly-dally on his homeward journey; Mary didn't delay until after supper to cast herself at His Feet; the Good Thief didn't let his conversion await upon Christ's descent from the Cross. Happiness and tranquillity are mine for the grasping. These days made miserable and dark by inner conflict and self-reproach so easily can end. . . .

The last notes of the Angelus have died on the still country air. Will I gain the indulgence now that the bell has stopped ringing? Well, anyway, "Angelus Domini nuntiavit Mariae. . . ."

I:00

"Breathes there a priest with luncheon fed, who never to himself has said, 'I think I'll take a little nap'?" Climbing the stairs seems to have aroused my poetic instincts—or maybe it's the altitude. Lapsing from poetry to prose as I kick off my shoes, it occurs to me that the subject of sacerdotal siestas is one that I never encountered in my pastoral theology books. Are they good or are they bad? Slothful self-indulgence or rational self-care? And just how long *is* a nap, anyway?

Flat on my back and gazing at the crack in the ceiling plaster, I am grateful that a doctor's orders have removed my own rest period from the tribunal of conscience. There was a time when I found the question of day-time sleep a disquieting problem, particularly as no authority seemed willing to say how much sleep a man needs. Eight hours, or seven, or six? "It's just a matter of habit," was the utmost commitment I could get from my own medico.

There are a few self-evident facts, of course, which need no scientific appraisal. Such as the fact that a healthy priest who goes back to bed after breakfast, is lying down in more ways than one; as is the priest who retires after lunch only to rise again in time for dinner. Surely it would be a defensible thesis to propose that anything more than eight hours repose in twenty-four is time stolen from God and one's people? The thesis would have as its major premise, that no honest parish priest can face God at any time of the day and say, "I've nothing to do."

The trouble begins (at least with me it did), with too many late evening hours given to personal pursuits. With the lights out in the parish office or the parish hall, there still would be time for a late visit to a friendly family, or a card-game at a neighboring rectory, or pleasurable-not-profitable reading into the wee small hours. Anything at all, rather than go to bed; after my long afternoon's repose, I was much too wakeful to retire. And so the vicious circle began, as habit fixed its form more firmly: too alert to sleep by night, too sleepy to labor by day.

The mattress is no respecter of persons in sounding its siren call. One would expect that some privilege be accorded to whitening hair and stiffening joints; but fully as many dark heads and ruddy cheeks will be found on daytime pillows, as furrowed brows and silver locks. It seems, indeed, that the ranks of the pathological sleepers are more youthful than aged—the pathological sleepers who seek surcease in their slumber rather than rest; self-made cataleptics who essay to escape their priesthood in sleep as others might in alcohol.

It is an insidious thing, I reflect (as I squirm my shoulders more comfortably into the inner-spring)—it is an insidious thing, this temptation to pamper oneself. It is so difficult to follow the golden mean between health preservation and sensual surrender. Certainly they are not heroes who burn themselves out betimes with long days and late nights of feverish activity, with nature's needs ignored. Their net gain is imperceptible if a case of jitters or a nervous stomach sends them off for a three months rest-cure.

For the average parish priest it seems impracticable to do one's duty by the evening's work, be up in time for one's morning meditation, and still get more than six hours or so of sleep. For such, an hour's mid-day rest would seem the part of prudence. It is not time stolen from God; the time already has been given to Him at either end of the day. The temptation to stretch that hour to two or three never can be a serious threat so long as that morning meditation gives joy in one's priesthood and strength for the day.

Now there's a funny thing . . . the crack in the plaster is beginning to waver . . . what was I thinking? . . . Oh yes; it's a funny thing, but when I prayed less I slept more, and never felt half so rested in the sleeping. Maybe I'm on to something there. Maybe that's why the saints could spend the night in prayer and still do a very good day's work. Maybe even my doctor could be wrong. Maybe. . . .

2:00

HERE IN THE COUNTRY the mailman comes but once a day. As I descend the stairs buttoning my cassock and blinking away the last remnants of my nap, I find today's accumulation of mail awaiting me: ads and bills and baptismal-certificate requests and marriage-notification forms and all the rest of it. It is willingly that I sit down at the desk for the task of winnowing; each batch of mail has a fascination of its own that never seems to pall. Good news or bad news or no news at all—there's adventure in each fresh stack of cancelled covers. Will this hand-addressed first-classer with no return address contain a check from some generous soul, or will it be a request that means a tedious search for a marriage record that isn't there? Even the unsealed envelope with a one-cent stamp and a printed legend, "Free Sample Inside," has its part in the picture, sucker-bait though I know it to be.

Near the bottom of the pile the familiar return-address of the Chancery Office looks up at me. What will it be this time? Another collection? Another regulation? Another . . . yes, it's another meeting; for all pastors and assistants, at two o'clock next Wednesday afternoon. A grunt of impatience escapes me. It will mean a seventy mile round-trip, a dollar's worth of gas, an afternoon's work lost while we listen to the reading of a paper that could just as well as not have been mailed to us in mimeographed form for perusal at home. Why can't Ordinaries be more *practical?*

But w-a-a-i-i-t a minute! How about this morning's meditation on the virtue of obedience and the Will of God? Didn't I give quick assent to the well-tried principles that *Obedience is better than sacrifice,* and *Not my will but Thine be done?* Didn't I agree whole-heartedly with the dictum that it is the *spirit* of obedience, and not mere external compliance, that makes for Christian and priestly perfection? Most certainly I did. And I felt quite pleased with myself as I speculated that one of the joys of the Beatific Vision will be the visible and magnificent harmony between the Divine Will and Christ's Human Will; between God's Will and the created wills of all the angels and saints, so perfectly reciprocal and so perfectly co-inciding. My fancy dwelt—I remember now—upon Hell as a place in which volitional conflict is of the very essence. I even titillated my imagination with a scene in which I escaped temptation because two competing devils were each determined that I should sin by *his* method or not at all.

Then there were the resolutions, so facilely formed: No further waste of energy and time (not to mention grace) spent in wondering why the Church demands this or insists on that. No more resentment at having to read the baptismal responses in Latin and answer them myself, while a line of nervous sponsors wait uneasily with their squalling babies. No more murmuring at having to sweat through the summer in black attire, while envying the missionaries their white. No more self-pity for my tiring feet as I read the Holy Saturday prophecies. Even in the littlest things I shall be obedient—so my resolution ran—even in the matter of wearing a biretta to and from the altar, even in giving the un-American-seeming kisses at a Solemn Mass.

Yes, my resolution was very thorough. Canons and rubrics and decrees, all were included. The will of my Ordinary too, whether manifested in command or merely in preference, whether personally or through delegates, *usque ad decanum*, all should have my assent, without question or remonstrance. My over-weening conceit, of course, will tell me that I could run the diocese better than the one whom the Holy Spirit has chosen for the task; it will tell me that all bishops are unjust and unreasonable by nature, and capricious by choice; it will assure me that the Holy Spirit has made His selections solely on the basis of providing the required daily cross for the Son's disciples. Admitting all this, I still cannot escape the meditation's inexorable conclusion: that every failure in obedience is a barrier between myself and Christ, a choking-off of grace at its very source.

But it has its difficulties, this inner obedience which conscience tells me I *must* embrace. There is the inevitable conflict between my own keenness of perception and the hidebound obtuseness of all the Roman congregations who legislate so freely for situations of which they have no personal experience. There is the inescapable consciousness of my own superior intelligence having to submit to the ineptness of diocesan officials, high and low. There is, in short, PRIDE, that arch-villain of a thousand faces, ably abetted in the pinches by Sloth, conspiring between them to destroy the spirit of obedience; even while they leave standing, as part of their conspiracy, the hollow shell of external observance.

So there is to be a meeting next week on Wednesday at 2:00 P.M. Very well, I'll be there. It is Christ Who calls me to the meeting, so I cannot well decline. It is Christ Who will take my place as pastor while I am away, doing more by His grace than I ever could accomplish in the same hours. As I renew my grasp upon the morning's resolutions, it is with a consciousness that obedience is a virtue that will flow and penetrate from above. If I can but make God's Will mine, in practice and in truth, then it is an obedient people that will follow me, their shepherd. Conflict stilled in my own heart, it shall be in peace and harmony that I shall lead my flock.

2:15

THE REST of the mail will have to wait. It is time now for the children's confessions, and I'll need a full seventy-five minutes for the forty or so who are waiting to go. Two minutes per child doesn't seem like very much time, but I can remember when anything less than sixty youngsters per minute had me worried for fear I was losing my grip.

Those were the days when I zipped through the Mass with swishing alb and a hand that fairly whistled as it cut the air above the Oblata; when I trotted along the communion rail with barely a caricature of a cross over the ciborium, mangling the *Corpus Domini* in more ways than one. Those, too, were the days when the slides of my confessional shivered and quivered as they beat a tattoo on busy Saturday nights.

A bit overdrawn, perhaps, but today's generation surely would have called me a "hot-rod." How the devil ever got me to thinking that there was anything admirable in speed, I'll never understand. It's easy enough to understand *why* he'd want me to think so. Satan and all his cohorts can't stem the flow of grace from the Sacraments, but he manages to neutralize a lot of their fruitfulness as they are administered by heedless hands.

Take confessions, for instance. I don't know when I

first woke up to the fact that I ought to be something more than a sacramental vending machine. A little glimmer of grace, I guess, in the morning's meditation. Anyway it did dawn on me, eventually, that "physician of souls" and "spiritual guide" are something more than mere phrases to be mouthed in a sermon on the Sacrament of Penance.

Of course I never failed to bear down hard on the penitent who was missing Mass habitually or running around with another man's wife. But with most of the pious souls it was easy to half-listen in comfortable drowsiness, wondering the while whether I'd get back to the rectory in time for the end of the ball game, or maybe trying to cook up an idea for Sunday's sermon.

As I kneel before the altar now for my "Come, Holy Ghost," I find myself speculating whether there'll be souls in Heaven on a lower step of glory than they should be, because they went to confession to me. I dare not even contemplate the possibility that someone may have missed completely, because I dozed when the saving word was needed.

A shifting of feet behind me reminds me that the children are waiting. One moment more, while I renew my determination not to take their peccadillos lightly. Here behind me are forty potential saints. God's grace will do the fashioning, but my hand must hold the chisel, to form or to mar. Never so eloquently as now can the heart of the priest speak—and be heard—to the heart of the child. Ten words here are better than a hundred in the classroom, better than a thousand from the pulpit.

Morning prayers missed every day? A quiet word about the value of one's morning offering, a quick picture of a wasted day, like home-work done with an empty fountain pen, takes but a few seconds. Childish thefts? The poverty of Jesus, toyless and candyless, may be the antidote. Anger? Maybe you're just kidding (you whisper), when you make the Stations and tell Jesus you'd like to help carry His Cross?

The first time I began giving the children capsules of counsel, the Sister was worried. They were in the box so long (almost two minutes) that she thought they must be messing up their act of contrition. The smiles on their faces as they tripped out of the confessional were too much for her curiosity. She asked one little girl (the Seal, did you say?) what kept her so long. "Father was telling me a story," was the answer she got.

As I rise now and duck through the curtain, the thought comes to me that perhaps the aimless and anemic piety of our "good" Catholics may be due to the routine confessions that they've been habituated to since childhood. I grin in the darkness as I think what a shock it would be to some weekly "distractions-in-prayers" penitent, if I were quietly to ask her, "Would you like to become a saint?" Come Saturday, I think maybe I'll try it.

Possibly there are some priests who recommend mental prayer to their penitents, but I haven't been one of the number. But now that I think of it, it's an idea worth trying. I wonder if I can find a book, keyed to the layman's life, that will do for him what Chaignon's meditations can do for the priest? A book like that, building solidly on fundamentals, might help to eliminate such scandals as weekly communicants who engage in racial discrimination, social injustice, political knavery.

But whoa, Betsy! These are the kids' confessions you're getting ready to hear. As I reach for the knob on the slide, I make a last determined effort to shove every-

(79)

thing else out of my mind. Fearful avowals will come to me: "I went to the bathroom in the alley." Scrambled acts of contrition will give constant variety: "I am hardly sorry for having offended Thee" and "I digest all my sins." But through it all, as at no other time, I shall feel close to my Master. Christ and His little ones! (Dear Lord, help me lead them to Thee.)

3:30

THE CHILDREN'S CONFESSIONS are finished, and the school-bus stands quietly trembling, awaiting its screaming and squirming load of precious freight. As I sit down to my interrupted task of mining the day's mail, the familiar return address of the St. Papagus Mission Society looks up at me as hopefully as a puppy with tail awagging. Will he get a pat on the head, or a push with my foot as I hurry on my way? Hardly the latter. It is notorious that almost any kind of an appeal signed, "Yours in Christ," will draw at least a dollar from the average priest's pocket.

But the St. Papagus outfit is a little different from the mine-run. They have several hundred missionaries at home and abroad. They need chapels, subsistence for nuns and catechists, funds for hospitals and dispensaries. They have the man-power, but they need more tools if that man-power is not to be wasted. As I read their latest brochure, describing their far-flung outposts in the battle for souls, there stirs in me a sense of shame at the thought of my own comfortable ministrations to the complacently saved.

No, the sense of shame goes deeper than that. It has its roots in my persistent effort to close my ears to the words of my Master, "Go, sell what thou hast, and give to the poor; and come follow Me." His voice is soft, but He *will* be heard; no chance for me to plead ignorance or inadvertence in my attachments to the good things of this world. His formula for perfection is plain enough. I can ignore it only at my own risk.

True enough, I haven't the vow of poverty. But Christ isn't talking about vows, He's talking about voluntary and whole-hearted conformity to Himself. True enough, I can get to Heaven just by keeping the Commandments, as Christ plainly said. But I didn't become a priest just to get to Heaven; I could have fulfilled that minimum much more easily as a bricklayer, with a wife and children like everyone else. But I chose to gamble for much higher stakes: some degree, at least, of sanctity; some degree, at least, of love and intimacy with Christ.

"Go, sell what thou hast and give to the poor!" Like the refrain of Poe's *Raven*, the words keep ringing in my ears as I look down the list of missionary needs. Three thousand dollars will build a chapel. Three thousand dollars is what I paid for my cottage at the beach, my cottage which I use about fifteen days a year, while my Lord in Uganda waits for a sheltering roof and a Holy Mount of Sacrifice. Four hundred dollars will provide a burse for the education of a native seminarian. Four hundred dollars is just about the extra amount I put in my new car; I ride now on satin seat-covers and listen to Bing as I drive, while a vocation goes begging in Dacca. Two hundred dollars will supply a dispensary in Tanganyika. Two hundred dollars is what I paid for my movie camera, an expensive toy which I need about as much as a duck needs an umbrella. But I shoot my kodachrome pictures, while missionaries cry for quinine and penicillin.

I'm not consciously acquisitive. At least it has never occurred to me to accuse myself of covetousness in confession. But the devil has his own methods of tangling me up in the dollar sign. There's the matter of security in my old age: "I don't want to be a burden to anyone." And so I discount Christ's Lilies-of-the-field parable about ninety per cent, and comfortably watch my bank-account grow.

Then there's that trip to Europe that I'm saving for. I want to see Lourdes and Fatima and Rome before I die. Perhaps our Blessed Mother *would* be honored more by a little chapel dedicated to her name in some Chinese village—but I'd miss that ocean voyage. Maybe I *could* wait and be content to view Europe from the vantage point of Heaven, but a fellow has to have something to look forward to, he has to have some fun. At least he does if he's going to continue to take the Gospel with a grain of salt.

"Go, sell what thou hast and give . . ." Will someone *please* shut off that record! Supposing I do enjoy the feel of a well-filled wallet, almost as much as a father with six hungry kids to feed; supposing I do enjoy slapping down a twenty-dollar bill with the dinner-check, while I twirl my liqueur glass between my fingers; supposing I do enjoy riding in the club car more than in the day coach—there's no sin in any of that. I'm not laying up a fortune. My will isn't going to cause any scandal when it's probated. And I never turn down any of these appeals. I always send a dollar, sometimes two, sometimes even five.

"The crumbs that fell from the rich man's table." What's this? A new voice adds itself to the penetrating words that I've been trying to beat down. The Gospel in counter-point, searching me out, leaving me no corner in which to defend myself: "Go, sell what thou hast . . .

and feasted sumptuously every day . . . come follow Me . . . thou didst receive good things in thy lifetime . . . they neither sew nor do they spin . . . there is fixed a great chaos . . . receive a hundredfold reward. . . ."

All right. *All right.* I know I can't say, "Shut up!" to the Gospel. I'll give it a try. Maybe I'll be surprised.

4:00

THE DESK has been cleared of mail. That is to say, the letters have been read and stacked with the other unanswered correspondence. Unless I get busy and answer some of them soon, I'll have no friends left in this world. But right now I must get out my New Testament and give it a quick look. Margie is due at any minute. Margie has been assigned the Gospel Study for this week's meeting of our Catholic Action leadership group, and is down for a four o'clock appointment so that I can help her to prepare it. She will be followed by Jean at four-thirty, whose assignment is to lead the discussion on the Mystical Body.

The urgent call of the Popes to Catholic Action, to a fuller participation of the laity in the apostolate of the Church, is a rallying-cry that may not be ignored. Yet, more and more I am inclining to think that the Jocist technique of leadership training is not the American answer. With all the zeal in the world, where is a pastor to find the time for the necessary spiritual, intellectual, and practical direction that will form the leaders we so badly need? Five hours of time each week is scarcely too much for a chaplain to give his group. Multiplying that by two, four, or six, according to the number of cells in a parish section, poses a physical impossibility to the pastor whose day already is filled with duties which may not be neglected. And the chaplain's job is not one for haphazard fulfillment; it must be done well, or it were better left undone.

Maybe the American answer will be diocesan schools for the training of lay leaders, to which each parish may send its most promising candidates, even as we send our candidates to the seminary. I do not know what the ultimate solution of our own hierarchy may be. Of this only am I sure: the appeal of the Jocist method of Catholic Action arouses in me the same sense of frustration as do so many other good, if lesser, causes. The Enthronement of the Sacred Heart, the Rosary Crusade, the Liturgical Revival, the rural-life movement in the country and the parochial social-action schools in the city: each of them in turn fires my imagination with its potential for good, then leaves me wilted as I look at a crowded engagement pad.

It is all very well to say, "Let something less important go." But what *is* of less importance? I cannot neglect the sick, Christ's sufferers. I cannot neglect the school-children, the lambs of my flock, and His. I cannot be superficial in convert instructions. I cannot brush off those who come, worried or in trouble, for advice and counsel. Even the physical administration of the parish plant is something I may not shirk, for all that repairs and purchasing and accounting bear but indirectly upon the salvation of souls. Perhaps I could abandon the parish societies and confraternities to their own devices, but they would quickly scatter without the priest. I should lose what contact I have with my adults; and the whole point of Catholic Action in Europe has been to put the priest back in touch with his people.

It is a dilemma, right enough; a dilemma in which the things I should like to do, are posed against the things I *must* do. But even as I contemplate the dilemma, the answer to it stirs and raises itself into my field of vision— the sword which will cut the seeming Gordian knot. It is not a new answer, of course. But it is an answer that is easily evaded or ignored in the hypertensive activity of the modern parish. It is the same answer that St. Bernard gave to Pope Eugene, when he warned Blessed Eugene of the danger of giving himself so completely to others as to have nothing of himself left for himself; the danger, as we'd say today, of spreading himself too thin.

The answer is *greater personal holiness*. It's a hard answer, at first glance; it's so much easier to work for others than to work on one's self. But it is the only answer for the harried priest who sees so much to be done, and so little time in which to do it. The movement has not yet been started (whether Catholic Action or any other) which will substitute for priestly sanctity. But priestly sanctity will substitute, in a pinch, for almost anything else.

Is it leaders we need? It is Christ Who calls His leaders, and the leaders will hear and answer when Christ is made visible in the life of a holy pastor. Is it love of the liturgy that we seek? The people will love the Mass and cherish the sacraments when reverent faith and deep love are evidenced in every gesture of the officiating priest. Is it social justice that we would promote, burning charity that we would inflame? Surely God's Word cannot pour from the overflowing heart of a truly Christlike priest fifty-two Sundays a year, without striking off some answering sparks!

All this I know. I know too that it is no defense for me

to hide behind the shibboleth of "sacristy priest." If by "sacristy priest" I mean "arm-chair" priest, then let me say so. But if by "sacristy priest" I mean a priest with a deep love for Christ in His Mysteries; a priest who spends as much time in church as in reading the daily paper and the weekly magazines—then I am talking about a man who will do more for God, in the final accounting, than the greatest go-getter ever to have his name in the diocesan weekly.

I squirm at the logic of it. I can see where it's leading, and it doesn't look good for me at all. But if it's got to be a choice between more prayer and mortification on the one hand, or more discouragement and frustration on the other, maybe I'd better let my knees take some of the strain off my heart. Well, there's Margie at the door. It's the Gospel for Pentecost that we're going to prepare together. "If anyone love Me . . . My Father will love him, and We will come to him and make Our abode with him. . . . Let not your heart be troubled, or be afraid." That says it, surely!

5:00

As I HANG up the phone, I reflect that not the least of God's actual graces to His priests are their clerical friends. Father Ted has just called to invite me to his Forty Hours closing next Tuesday night. *Deo volente*, I'll most certainly be there. For me, such occasions are not lightly to be missed. How I do love the fellowship and the friendly banter; the atrocious insults that conceal friendly affection; the tongue-in-cheek praise that helps to keep one's feet upon the ground.

The usual crowd will be there: witty and talkative Dave, who is the world's surest cure for the blues; quick and excitable Don, who will argue heatedly about my right to bump the pot a nickel, but would give me his last dollar if I needed it; quiet and sensible Pete, with a solid shoulder to cry on when griping is the order of the day; easy-going, there's-always-tomorrow Ray, to make one's worries seem picayune and silly. They'll all be there, and a few others besides; each making his own particular contribution to the unique fraternity which is known to no other body of men in the world.

There'll be bottles on the sideboard, and ice and glasses. We'll pour a libation before sitting down to the housekeeper's annual culinary triumph. I'll look around the table at the faces that have been aging, with mine, through the years. With a sense of brotherhood that is never stronger than at a Forty Hours dinner, I'll be thinking again how much akin to the ancient Agape this meal must be.

With loosened belts we'll move into the living-room, where the conversation will rise and fall, alternating between the trivial and the serious. There'll be discussion of vacation plans, maybe, and someone's tough marriage case, and probable diocesan appointments, and current building programs, and all the rest that goes to make up a clerical bull session. Then at ten to eight we'll hoist ourselves to don cassocks and surplices and troop over to the sacristy with breviaries in hand. (The visiting missionary, as usual, will preach to the accompaniment of rustling leaves, stealthily turned.)

We'll find our places in the sanctuary, kneeling on the hard floor because there aren't enough prie-dieux to go around. Father Joe or maybe Jim will lead in the telling of the beads. The missionary will deliver his sermon, and there'll be a bit of a mechanical ring to it because he's given it so often. Jerry, the perennial chanter of the crowd, will intone the litany, and there'll be the slightly ragged chorus of responses in tenor, bass and baritone.

Then down the aisle we'll go, leading Him Whom at other times we so stumblingly follow. We'll spill wax on our cassocks, and proceed by fits and starts as the Holy Name men squeeze their way through the narrow side aisles. We'll be a motley-looking group, with our heads of black or grey (or bald); tall and short, fat and lean. But we'll thrill with a common heart to the faith of the congregation, and we'll think, like absent parents, of our own flock back home; wondering the while whether we have been giving them our best. We'll feel an unaccustomed sense of compunction at our derelictions, and we'll return through the altar gates with a renewed avowal of loyalty to the Master of Whom we are, so literally, the Body-guard. And as He turns, in the hands of the Dean, to impart His benediction, we'll pray, each of us, that His blessing may not stop within the walls of this church, but that His compassionate eyes may be also upon our own people, to remedy by His grace what we have so ill performed in our frailty.

"Holy God we praise Thy Name" will ring out fit to make the votive-lights dance in their sockets, and we'll be back in the rectory, momentarily subdued by the thoughts we have thought and the grace that has touched our hearts. But the tempo of talk will quickly pick up, and the cards and chips will come out for the game of five-and-ten which will round out the evening. Perhaps the folks who saw us gathered half an hour ago around the altar might be surprised to see us now gathered around the green table. But as I glance at the faces about me, relaxed for the moment from the cares that were, today, and will be, tomorrow;—as I glance at their faces I'll recall again, with the knowledge of close friendship, their dogged perseverance and self-conquests through the years; their fidelities which ever have been stronger than their weaknesses; their hidden love which far outweighs their lapses. Remembering, I'll feel proud again to be one of them—proud, and humbly grateful. And, oddly enough, I'll feel confident that Christ still is in the midst of us.

It will be midnight, next Tuesday, before I turn my car homeward, probably with beer on my breath. I'll be well aware that I haven't spent the evening in the company of saints; else I should never have felt so much at home. I'll realize quite clearly that it would be better if we all *were* saints, and spent the evening in pious converse and abstemious simplicity. But we aren't, and we won't. Yet there's grace of another kind in their companionship. Through the months and the years, my priest friends have been the cloud by day and the pillar of fire by night which have kept me, under God, inching forward.

Now, as I pick up my breviary to anticipate, the memory of Father Zeke intrudes itself into my thoughts. Father Zeke never cared much for clerical gatherings or the company of priests. He said they drank too much, and talked too much nonsense; they had no conception of the seriousness of their calling. Well, Father Zeke wears a necktie now, and is a father-in-fact. Maybe he'd have cracked anyway; God forbid that I should judge. But I'm going to offer Matins and Lauds for him, with a concurrent intention of gratitude to God for the friends who have helped to keep me where I am.

6:15

No DOUBT my parishioners (especially the ones who live seven and eight miles from church) would be amazed to know how difficult it is for me to get in my daily visit to the Blessed Sacrament. So difficult in fact that sometimes my thanksgiving after Mass is the last I see of the sanctuary until next morning's meditation. Right next door to the church, too! The difficulty can't be anything else but subjective. The incongruity of it all never even occurred to me until the last time I preached a Forty Hours. Right in the midst of a grand and orotund appeal for frequent visits to Jesus in the tabernacle—just as I was weeping over the tepidity of human hearts and the pity of it all—a nasty little voice piped up somewhere inside me: "Listen, buddy, if your medicine is so good, why don't you take it yourself?" From there on I hurried to a ragged conclusion.

With Matins anticipated and dinner eaten, right now I've got a spare quarter-hour before my next appointment at 6:30. So here I am in church, and glad to be here, once I accomplished the heroic bypassing of the evening paper. Glad to be here because I have somewhat to talk over with my Lord. A little matter of mental depression that seems to have settled upon me as the day has waned.

Something that I can't quite put my finger on, although I can trace some of its causes.

It started with Sister Principal's phone call at five o'clock, to tell me that the Karnicks are taking their children out of our school, because of the Negro girl that we just admitted to our seventh grade. That means an unpleasant visit to the Karnicks' home without much hope of success; I know how stubborn they both can be. And I'll worry about their youngsters being in the public school and themselves being resentful perhaps, and myself helpless because I cannot make the Charity of Christ more vivid to them than their own prejudices.

And then just as dinner was on the table came Mrs. Knowles in tears, bearing in her hand an anonymous letter that she received today. It's quite evidently from one of her neighbors and fellow-parishioners, and packs a venom and a malice that almost is shocking. The worst of it is that aside from the bitterness and distortion of the letter, most of what it says is true. I sent her home comforted to a degree, but it has left me uneasy that one of my flock could write in such a vein.

Yes, there were these things; added to the natural wear and tear of the day, they probably account for the blue mood that has come to me. It is a blue mood not wholly new. It has come at other times and from other causes. There is that sagged-shoulder feeling, the temptation to wonder whether it's worth the struggle, whether I'm really getting anywhere, whether I wouldn't have been better off as a married man with a nice easy job like a city fireman. It doesn't often get that bad, of course. Usually I just begin to think longingly of cloisters and monasteries, suddenly discovering in myself an unsuspected vocation to the religious life with someone else bearing the burdens and doing the worrying, while all I'd have to do would be to answer the bells. In my saner moments, of course, I recognize that for the pipe-dream it is. I know there's no cloister I can hie to, no hole I can crawl into, where I won't have to carry myself with me. Common sense tells me there are probably as many blue moments in monastic cells as in pastoral studies.

It is a message something like that which is trying to get through to me now, as I kneel quietly looking at the tabernacle, not saying anything, just letting it sink into me that Christ is really and personally there; letting build up in myself the stark truth (so fuzzy most of the time because so familiar) that Christ is *really there.* It's not just a holy thing I'm looking at, a bronze safe for the protection of a sacred sacrament, not a numinous Presence, august and impersonal, to Whom I am an expendable mote of dust; CHRIST IS THERE!

I've got it now. Not for long, I know. But just for this minute He's as real to me as He must have been to Lazarus, stumbling confusedly from the tomb. My eyes begin to smart, and I feel like crawling on my knees to the altar and laying my head on the mensa; only I know it wouldn't get me any closer than I am. And my depression drains from me like pus from a punctured abscess. Christ's healing Love has penetrated the tough hide of my self-love and my self-pity.

The answers were there all the time, only now I can read them. What do I mean, "Is it all worth while?" Worth while from the viewpoint of other blind fools like yourself, or worth while from My viewpoint, son? It's worth Eternity, it's worth Me. Is there anything more that you want? Every weary failure which you encounter is a part of My pattern; every blind alley that you follow is a road to Me. You just keep plugging along, son, and let Me reap the fruit My own way.

And don't forget this, Trese, My disciple: for all that you're so weak and so inert; for all that you're so soft and all-but-impervious to My tempering; for all that you're so complacent in your sins; for all that I've had to pour out more grace upon you than I ever spared to Judas—I still love you, My boy, and you'll not lose Me nor I you until you stand up and throw My love back in My Face.

It doesn't sound very biblical, but that's how it came through to me. Anyway, the moment is ended. Tomorrow my Visit probably will be very pedestrian. And the day after, too; and the day after that. But sometime there'll be another moment like the one that's just gone. I'll have to keep coming every day to make sure I'm here when it happens.

6:30

As I step out of the sacristy door, I see Frank Smith ringing the rectory doorbell, punctually on time for his instruction. His battered jalopy stands at the curb, loaded with his only treasures—his wife and baby on the front seat, and four tousled heads behind. Apparently the whole family is going shopping tonight, as soon as I finish with Frank. Four hands wave at me as I go up the steps to join their father, and again I feel that twinge of envy that the childless so often feel in the presence of a happy family.

It is a twinge that is only momentary, of course. Common sense quickly reminds me of the high price that Frank is paying for his family. I know something of his heart-aches and worries, his doing-without and his making-do, his sleepless nights and his nightmares of insecurity. I know of the youngster he lost, and of the doctor bills he's paying off month by month.

Who am I, dear God, to take pride in my vow of chastity! There was a time, in my simplicity, when I thought that it was something grand that I was giving to You, while the truth of it is that it is something You have graciously given to me. Now that I think of it, it seems strange that men should honor us most (even when they do so grudgingly and suspiciously) for that which is the least of our burdens.

Perhaps I might make more progress in other virtues, if I would remind myself more often of what a little thing this vow of chastity is. Perhaps I might labor more diligently at the work of my sanctification, if I did not so complacently assume salvation merely because I have renounced, freely, what so many less fortunate men have had to renounce through circumstance.

It is a perilous privilege, this celibacy. It is so easy for me loftily to assume a heroism I do not really possess, the while I fail in virtues that would make me truly priestly. It is so easy to be chaste yet cantankerous, pure yet proud, celibate yet slothful.

I don't suppose that any priest has ever yet fallen from his high estate because of the crushing pressure of his vow. One cannot fall from a height which he has already abandoned. And that height seldom is surrendered in one dramatic gesture. Rather it is a sly and slow descent, with self-love the motivating force.

It is my self-love, dear God, and not my procreative faculty, upon which Your grace must labor hardest. I do so love my ease, and it is not easy to pray, so I shall do anything rather than pray. By a queer contradiction of sloth, I shall even work my head off rather than pray. I shall go to bed at night thoroughly exhausted because I have been running away from You all day long; and I shall fall asleep blindly confident of having spent the day in Your service.

By a very refinement of sloth, even my choice of tasks is such as will minister most to self. I shall find a dozen trifling duties at my desk, rather than go out to punch doorbells and round up the strays. I shall spend an hour mending a broken lock or a frayed toaster-cord, rather than pay a call on old bed-ridden O'Connor in his filthy shack. I shall run my legs off getting uniforms or getting games for our parish athletes, rather than prepare a heel-rocking talk on the lay apostolate that might rouse them from their good-paganism.

Self-love will carefully cherish comfort, too. There is no comfort in mortification, so mortification must join prayer in exile. Health requires that I get my needed rest, even if I must rush from pillow to predella, unshaven and unrecollected. My nerves would suffer if I were to quit smoking, my strength might wane unless I ate heartily, my physical tone might decline unless I did recreate generously.

And then there is poverty, mortification's alter-ego. Poverty easily is out-foxed by pride. Or is it covetousness? Is it covetousness, Lord, or is it childishness, that I must have the best and the latest in cars, and in television, and in air-conditioning, and in all the other gadgets with which a secular world tries to fill the void that was You?

Well, there is always tomorrow. Yet in my moments of honesty I know that already there have been too many tomorrows, and that tomorrow it will be tomorrow still. I know too that if ever I collapse (which may Your mercy forbid!) it will not be through the onus of my vow. The capitulation of that citadel would be but the surrender of an empty and a ruined city. Before it can fall, so much that is more vital must first have been jettisoned. Help me, dear Lord, to make tomorrow today!

7:30

THE MARKS FAMILY is due at seven-thirty, but there will be plenty of time for me to answer a letter or two from my stock of neglected correspondence. The Markses always are late, which is understandable, considering that there are six of them. They are coming corporately into the Church, including little Doreen who is four, and the baby who sleeps so unabashedly through my explanations of the Creed.

It was a happy grace that led me to call on them some three months ago. Philip, the father, had come to the kitchen door to borrow the use of the phone that he might call a doctor for his sick wife. The housekeeper (the F. B. I. of every rectory) gathered from his talk with the doctor, that he was out of work and low on funds. She so reported at the supper table, and when I passed Marks's house the next day, I stopped in to see if I could proffer any help. Not being Catholics, they were all a bit self-conscious at the presence of a priest, and the baby cried at the sight of me. But they all crowded around the door to see me off, after politely assuring me that they were getting along all right.

A month or more later thirteen-year-old Sarah stopped in to say that she'd never been baptized, and her mother said she should be, and would I baptize her? It wasn't quite as simple as that, I explained: her parents would have to consent to her becoming a Catholic, she'd have to take instructions. . . . Well, anyway, in another six weeks the Markses all will be gathered around the font, to become members of Christ's Mystical Body.

It is strange, now that I think of it, that it took me so long to realize in empiric fashion that all souls within my boundaries are members of my parish. In theory I always knew it, of course. But it was several years before I began to remember very especially in my Masses the non-Catholic members of my flock. It is even more tardily that I have developed an attitude of mind whereby, as I shake hands with the local Methodist minister, I see in him one of "mine," for whom I shall one day have to answer.

It has made a difference, this revised appraisal of my non-Catholic parishioners as being potential pew-holders rather than adamant adversaries. It is a state of mind that seems to lubricate my approach to them. They seem to sense a genuineness of interest and sincerity of purpose which was far absent from my let's-observe-the-social-decencies-but-keep-at-your-distance relationship of other days. Nowadays I feel almost as worried, when one of my non-Catholics marries a divorcee or is killed suddenly in an accident, as though the same thing had happened to a registered parishioner.

Not worried for them, so much as for myself. I'm not doing for them as much as I ought. As much, that is, in the way of prayer and penance. Those, after all, are the only two tools that I have to work with. I have not the gift of eloquence which overpowers, nor the magnetic personality which charms. I haven't even time—time for all the promotional mechanics recommended by the books on effective convert-making. But I *could* pray more, and I *could* practice greater mortification, to win the graces that my flock, whether in or out of the fold, so sorely need. I've never yet voiced an urgent prayer coupled with an act of self-denial, that I haven't been able to trace the results. Sometimes results so fruitful as almost to be startling, like dropping a nickel absently into a slot machine and hitting the jack-pot.

Probably most other priests have come to realize much more quickly what I have been so slow to see: that it is the holy priest, and not the "big-operator," whose apostolate is the most fruitful. Fruitful, that is, in the long pull. Fruitful through the years, like seed planted deep whose roots mature slowly but last on and on.

Maybe it's not wisdom but just my gray hairs that foster these musings. Maybe it's not the beginnings of piety, but a sort of tiredness that inspires these reflections. It is true, certainly, that as we grow older we priests can easily grow a bit cynical. So often we have seized upon the latest panacea for the reform of faith and morals; so often we have grasped fervidly at the newest scheme for transforming our parishes; only to see (we or our successors) the frenzy spend itself, enthusiasm die, and ourselves back where we started.

So we come, surely not mistakenly, to lean more and more heavily upon the grace of God. Or rather, we finally perceive the truth that was staring us in the face all the time—that all the while we thought we were moving mountains, it was God's Little Finger, fulcrumed by somebody's prayer and somebody's penance, that actually was doing the work.

Anyway it is a comfort, as the years slow us up, to understand at last that there is a short cut—that more time spent before the altar and less indulgence given to self will accomplish what no corresponding amount of activity ever could achieve. It is a comfort to look around us with our newly-unfilmed eyes, and see that it is the truly good priests, moving with kindness and gentleness and patience and unaffected friendliness among their flocks, who are the shepherds, spiritually speaking, of the fattest folds.

Well, I hear a clatter of footsteps upon the porch, so the Markses are here. The pen in my hand hasn't even touched itself to the first of the two letters I was going to write. And in spite of my reverie, tomorrow or the next day I'll probably read of some fool-proof scheme for making my parish into a communion of saints, and proceed to work myself into a lather trying it out, and once again the balance of *ora et labora* will dip heavily towards the longer word.

8:30

WITH A HOPE—somewhat forlorn—that the evening may be free from further interruptions, I settle to the task of preparing that talk for Sunday's meeting of the Altar Society. This is Friday night, and a busy Saturday isn't going to allow much time for quiet thought and recollection.

As I zip a sheet of paper into the typewriter, the absurdity of what I'm doing suddenly is borne in upon me. Here I am, about to think out carefully a talk for maybe a hundred women; taking pains, because it's a bit of a special occasion, this meeting Sunday afternoon. And yet on Sunday morning I'll be facing a total audience of at least a thousand people, and up to this moment I haven't been a bit concerned with what I'm going to say to them.

There'll be a thousand faces looking up at me as I mount the pulpit. Some of them will be faces heavy with care, waiting for a word of strengthening hope to help them through another hard week. There'll be bored faces, too—the faces of the lukewarm who long since have made comfortable compromise with the world and the flesh, not asking for anything except to be left undisturbed in their atrophy. There'll be stubborn faces there, sullen façades behind which lie habits of accepted and established sin, daring me to penetrate their self-willed deafness if I can. Sprinkled everywhere there'll be the fresh faces of the future, the children waiting for the story that will stick in their minds, ready to withdraw into their own dream-world the moment I begin to multiply the syllables.

Hopeful, indifferent, antagonistic, a thousand pairs of eyes will be challenging me. It will be the opportunity of a life-time, even though by the grace of God it is an opportunity that will be repeated week after week. The chance of a life-time, to convert even one sinner, to fire even one soul to sanctity. And I haven't even begun to think of what I'm going to say. If it were a talk for the Rotary Club, with forty well-fed stomachs lending a haze to my words; or if it were a baccalaureate sermon which no one ever remembers, I'd have been sweating over it these two weeks past. But an ordinary Sunday sermon for my people . . . for *my people* . . . "those whom Thou hast given me" . . . for them I can throw a few words together in the course of my Saturday night shower.

There is a defense, of course—a false Maginot sort of defense behind which I've been resting too long. "My real preparation for preaching was made in the Seminary," the argument runs; "and all I need now is a little last-minute brushing up on the Gospel of the day. I've got all the dogma and moral and Scripture that my people can handle, right at my finger-tips." Then the years have brought an auxiliary argument: "I've been a priest so long that the old truths rise easily (and cornily) to my lips." And of course there is always the clincher, the argument irrefutable: "What's the use of beating your brains out for a lot of people with one foot in the aisle, just waiting to get home for Sunday dinner?"

Even as I marshal them, I can see all these old bulwarks

to my sloth crumbling. All the unprepared after-dinner speeches through which I've ever squirmed now rise up to remind me that grammar and smooth, confident delivery do matter; all the effective speakers who have ever held me spellbound now rise up to tell me that apt anecdote and pertinent story and freshness of treatment make all the difference in the world.

And as I look at the still-blank paper in my typewriter, another figure takes shape to warn me that even these mechanics are not enough. It is the figure of the Curé of Ars, standing at the vestment case in his sacristy, laboriously writing out his sermons with one eye on the sanctuary lamp. There is where I have failed, far more lamentably than in art of pen or tongue. How little I have prayed over what I have spoken! What small part the Holy Ghost has had in my words! How little conscious I have been that preaching—and not athletics nor dances nor bingo—is one of the three great powers and privileges of my priesthood. Is it any wonder that I haven't straightened the stooped shoulders of the discouraged? Is it any wonder that I haven't jarred the sinner from his apathy? Is it any wonder that I haven't doubled Holy Communions and filled the church for weekday Mass?

It's time that I quit confusing a facile tongue and a readiness in speech, with the power of the Holy Spirit. It's time that I quit telling myself that I could be a Monsignor Sheen, too, if only I had the leisure to polish up my talks. It's time long past (and Oh! for the wasted years!) that I began putting some prayer and perspiration into my sermons, let bingo and basketball fall where they may. Over to church with me now, for a prayerful session with Sunday's Gospel; then back to my typewriter for a crack at a *real* Sunday sermon. Let the good ladies of the Altar Society take their chances.

9:30

THE OUTLINE for Sunday's sermon is finished. At least, I've jotted down a few thoughts which I can be chewing on between now and Sunday. They will be better, surely, than the few fuzzy platitudes I so often garner in the ten minutes preceding Mass.

My text shall be "If anyone love Me, he shall keep My word, and My Father will love him, and We shall come to him." It seems as good a text as any for a sermon on the Sacrament of Penance as a means of sanctification and a bond of more intimate union with God. Point one will be a more careful and honest examination of conscience, and none of this, "Father I don't remember any sins since my last confession." Point two will be more attention to the motives for true sorrow, and none of this rattling off of the act of contrition as though it were a magical incantation. Point three will be more sincerity in the purpose of amendment, and none of this repetition of the same old faults in the same old number week after week.

As I count the points off on my fingers, there comes to me an uninvited vision of my own confession, when I pay my weekly visit to old Father Brady tomorrow morning. I'll drive over to his rectory with my mind, as usual, busy about everything except the sacrament which I am going to receive. I'll ring his door-bell without first stopping for a moment at his church. We'll smoke a cigarette together and pass the time of day. Then he'll get out his stole and I'll drop to my knees and we'll go through the same old routine again. He knows already what I'm going to say; I doubt whether he even seriously listens any more. I know what his own little ferverino will be, but I'll bow my head piously while he says it. The only thing that saves the whole procedure from being a total loss is the fact that I am—I hope—genuinely sorry for the sins of my past life. So there will be at least a little grace forthcoming from the bountiful mercy of God; more than I'm entitled to, all things considered.

But it isn't Father Brady, God love him, who is to blame for the meagerness of fruit, nor for my smug content at having discharged a weekly duty. It's just that he's too old in the priesthood, and too wise in the ways of us, to elaborate on the essentials of the sacrament. He wouldn't dream of putting it into words—probably wouldn't even formulate the thought—but in his heart he knows that I don't really want the kick in the pants that I ought to have.

He knows I don't really want him to say, "Listen, Father; these distractions in Divine Office you mention every week: how much of your Office do you say in church, while you let the housekeeper take care of the phone and the doorbell—and the radio?" He knows I don't really want him to say, "This missing of your spiritual reading which you speak of: would you mind telling me how much time you spent this past week on *Time*, and *Reader's Digest*, and that murder-mystery I noticed by your chair the other day?"

He knows I don't want him to say, "These uncharitable and critical remarks that you include in every week's confession: have you ever tried to get to the root of them? Is there any jealousy or envy there, which would be the *real* sin? How do you feel about that classmate of yours that was made a monsignor last week? Did it make you wince a bit?" He knows I don't want him to say, "About this 'vanity and self-complacency' that you always include at 'once or twice a week': do you just throw that in to make yourself feel piously humble, or do you really understand what it means to rob God of His glory?"

He knows I don't want him to say, "You always make a vague reference to 'graces I've failed to correspond to.' Let's get our heads out of the clouds and sink our teeth into something. Just what graces *have* you failed to correspond with, and why haven't you?" He knows I don't want him to say, "My son, you made the same confession today that you made a year ago. If you were a better priest, you'd have more to tell, because your conscience would be more tender. But they wouldn't be the same faults and the same number of times over and over again. There'd be some change because there'd be some progress."

My confessor knows all this. He knows that I don't really want to be a saint, and he knows he can't carry my dead weight up the ladder all alone. *He* knows that *I* know all the answers as well as he does. He knows that I can't be saved from my own mediocrity without effort on my part, any more than a drunk can be saved from his alcoholism without the will to fight.

He knows all this, does old Father Brady, and I haven't a doubt that he's watched me down his steps many a time, with a prayer that the grace of the sacrament might in time open my eyes to the practice of what, come Sunday, I'm going to preach.

(109)

10:30

As THE MANTEL CLOCK strikes the half-hour, I lay aside Abbé Trochu's *The Curé d'Ars*, my current spiritual reading. Much as I hate to leave good St. John Vianney in the midst of one of his bouts with Satan, duty calls elsewhere. I am grateful, as it is, for an unusually quiet hour, interrupted only twice by phone and door-bell.

Now I must hie me to the parish hall and look in on the young folks at their weekly dance. Look in just long enough to smile and bob my head a few times as the kids flit by, and return a wave of the hand to the more distant ones. Look in just long enough to remind them that there is a tie-in between their dance and their God, and maybe turn a mind or two from the lure of a parked car at intermission time.

As I walk over to the hall, I mull over again the prob-lem that is a constant torment to us priests—the problem of how to be the spiritual men we *must* be, in the face of all the extra-sacerdotal activities we have to engage in. It must have been wonderful, in the days and in the countries where the governments footed all the bills, and where every school was a Catholic school. It must have been wonderful to have had nothing to do but pray, and visit the sick, and preach, and teach catechism, and seek out the stray sheep.

But today we build our own churches and pay our own salaries and build parochial schools in expensive competition with free-handed politicians. Today we must have elaborate recreational programs for our youth, to keep them parish-centered, with a strong social pressure from within to resist the terrific social pressure from without. To pay for it all we must have bingoes and raffles and bazaars, until we find ourselves thinking of the parish bank-balance far more often than we think on the Four Last Things. Maybe there's a new era coming. Maybe Catholic Action and the Lay Apostolate will make things easier for the next generation. But darn it, I don't belong to the next generation; time's running out fast for me.

No saints, no saints. Every year the Pope canonizes Italians and Frenchmen and Portuguese, but the only American saint we've got had to be born and bred in Italy. Of course there's a bright side to the picture, too. It almost seems that saints are born of God's necessity to combat evil. The great wonder-workers arise when all else about them seems to be on the road to hell. Maybe there's comfort in the fact that we haven't any American saints; maybe we aren't bad enough yet to need them.

No doubt other priests, too, get discouraged at the mediocre level of sanctity in their parishes. Especially when they reflect, as I do in my lucid moments, that the pastor is the pattern of his flock. Especially when they encounter, as I do again and again, crescent saints in the fold, who are quietly forming their own pattern of sanctity without benefit of oneself. Especially when they look back along the path, as I so often find myself doing, and see the series of shattered resolutions. Meditation, mortification, spiritual reading, nobly instituted and soon neglected; begun again and once more forgotten; determination so firm and perseverance so flabby. Well, I suppose the important thing is to keep pushing, pushing, pushing. Two steps forward and one step back.

Anyway we do fill our churches on Sunday. And the men come as well as the women. As the first strains of the dance-band strike my ear, I reflect that these dancing kids, a lot of them, will be at Holy Communion Sunday. As I mount the steps and the first whiff of powder and perfume tickles my nostrils, an impish thought comes to me: Maybe we Americans are like the saints whom the Breviary finds so hard to classify, and who are lumped solemnly under the title of "Neither Virgins Nor Martyrs." And an absurd vision rises before my eyes: A vision of St. Peter showing a visitor through Heaven, pointing out reverently the mansions of the holy pastors of souls, the doctors and the confessors and the apostles and the abbots; and coming finally to a blissful throng, looking still a bit harried in their happiness, with halos definitely ill-fitting. And St. Peter, not quite able to conceal his own puzzled wonderment, pointing them out to the visitor: "These are the American priests." God grant that I may be among them!

11:30

SITTING ON THE EDGE of the bed winding the alarm, I reflect again—as I do every night at this time, except sometimes it's later—I reflect again that I could have been sound asleep by now if I hadn't dawdled so. But the dawdling is one of those little luxuries that I love. There's no peace, on the human level, like the peace that comes with the shutting of one's bedroom door upon the day's cares. It may be true in some places that a man's home is his castle, but not in a rectory, where a man lives with his work through all his waking hours. In the seminary, I used to picture myself as a priest, relaxed in my study with a pipe and a good book. I know now that that is a picture strictly for the movies. My good books and clerical reviews are mostly scattered helter-skelter about the house—office, living-room, dining-room, bedroom—wherever I have been lucky enough to find a spare moment or two.

Off with the light and up with the blanket. A final quick check in the sudden darkness: yes, I said my night prayers; yes, I said my rosary this morning; yes, I finished my Office; yes, I locked all the doors and switched the phone and doorbell upstairs. . . . Through the open window comes the soft hoot of a distant train. In the creek across the road my bullfrog friend tunes up his bass.

Duke, on my neighbor's farm, barks sharply twice at a fancied shadow. All of them sounds that I love, all of them signals that the curtain is dropping on another day.

Not a big day, not an important day, like the day the Cardinal came for our Centennial, or the day our first school bus brought in its first load of kids for their first day in a Catholic school. Just routine today, with the usual proportion of ups and downs. And tomorrow will be like it, only different duties and different problems and different faces. But the same me.

That's it: the same me. Now in the darkness, as I wait for the drowsiness and the quick black-out, I can face it. The same me, yesterday, today and forever. Talking big and acting little. Talking big to myself, that is. I'm going to be a real man of prayer, soon. I'm going to start practicing real mortification any day now. I'm going to be a wholly pliable tool in the Hands of God for the revitalizing of my people, and leave my parish a parish of saints.

Phooey on me! Out of the past comes my mother's weary voice: "Leo, you're always saying, 'I was just going to'; sometimes I wish you'd say, 'I just did.'" When they plant a stone over me, they can carve on it, "He was a great kidder—of himself." I might even claim, if a statesman hadn't beaten me to it, the title of Great Compromiser. In me the lion and the lamb have lain down together: charity and self-love; penance and comfort; prayer and worldliness; humility and pride.

But my mother was patient, I remember. Patient to the very end, when she motioned for a drink of water, and I jumped and said, "I was just going to . . .", and she smiled weakly and blessed me with the smile.

The drowsiness is thickening my wits fast now, but I must follow that thought to the end. . . . My Master is patient too. He was so patient with John and James. So patient with Peter. Patient with Judas too. It was a big sin that Judas did when he betrayed my Lord; but a bigger sin by far when he gave up hope, when he quit trying.

Somehow God will fit this day (I raise my head from the pillow to halt the drop into oblivion) somehow God will fit this day into His Plan. He fitted the Pharisees in, and the Sanhedrin, and Judas even. But he fitted the Magdalen in, too, and Saul and Augustine. Surely somewhere in between He can find a place for me and my foolishness and my weakness and my pettiness. Maybe I *shall* face Him in Judgment with a shamefaced, "I was just going to." But His grace will not cease working so long as I do not cease trying. Perhaps even yet I shall come up, flushed and breathless, with "I just did." Anyway, tomorrow will be another . . . tomorrow will be . . . tomorrow. . . .